DON'T JUDGE
MY FUTURE
BY MY PAST

DON'T JUDGE MY FUTURE BY MY PAST

Dennis Leonard

DON'T JUDGE MY FUTURE BY MY PAST

Dennis Leonard
9495 East Florida Avenue
Denver, CO 80247
(303) 369-8514
www.dennisleonardministries.com

ISBN 1-880809-15-X
Printed in the United States of America
© 2003 by Dennis Leonard

Legacy Publishers International
1301 South Clinton Street
Denver, CO 80247
www.legacypublishersinternational.com

Cover design by: Nikki Braun

1 2 3 4 5 6 7 8 9 10 / 09 08 07 06 05 04

CONTENTS

DEDICATION

I would like to give special thanks to my wonderful wife, Michele, for helping me to prepare and complete this book. And most of all, for her love that has brought tremendous healing to my life.

And finally, thank you to the family of Heritage Christian Center for loving me in spite of my past and my failures.

Bishop Dennis Leonard

FOREWORD
BY BISHOP EDDIE LONG

D ue to the process of life, we can become discouraged and every once in a while need to be reminded of God's deliverance. The message of healing, deliverance, restoration, and victorious Christian living that God has placed in Bishop Dennis Leonard, is a timely message to this generation, particularly in this new millennium.

Bishop Leonard is gifted and called of God to bring this message to the Body of Christ. In a straightforward style that is easy to understand, Bishop Leonard explains the process of being healed from our pasts and propelled toward our eternal destiny. This book is a challenge to the faith of every believer, especially those of Heritage Christian Center, the house he shepherds in Denver, Colorado.

Many in the Body of Christ would rather cover up the broken and cracked areas of their lives, but this man of God understands that true healing and God-ordained destiny is determined by our willingness to deal with our pasts. I pray that as you read these pages, the healing power and presence of Almighty God would rest upon you.

I am truly convinced that Bishop Dennis Leonard is a gift to the Body of Christ. I guarantee that everyone who reads this book will experience healing and victory because of one man's willingness to be obedient to the call of God.

Bishop Eddie Long, D.D., D.H.L.
Senior Pastor
New Birth Missionary Baptist Church

INTRODUCTION

The Bible says that all have sinned and fallen short of the glory of God. In other words, no matter who we are, we've had failures in the past. But as long as you live in the past, you'll never have much of a future. The purpose of this book is to help you overcome all of your sins, all of your failures, and all of your past mistakes.

Whether you were abused or you were the abuser, God wants to help you build a new life. Whether you were raised in a wonderful family or a family that neglected you, God wants to help you conquer every enemy in the past, present, and future. With God's help, you can get your past behind you and start over today.

If your past keeps haunting you, then it is time to trust the Lord with all of your heart and lean not on your own understanding. If your past is trying to hold you back, you must stop dwelling on your failures and let God take you into the promised land.

Yes, we've all had failures in the past, but just because we have failed in the past doesn't mean we will fail in the future. Don't judge my future by my past because it's a new day in the Lord. Yes, I have had some failures, but that was then and this is now. I am starting a new life with the Lord's help.

God bless you,
Bishop Dennis Leonard

DON'T JUDGE MY FUTURE BY MY PAST

Chapter One

STUCK IN THE PAST

Are you satisfied with your life today? Are you moving forward in confidence, enjoying each new development as it comes your way? Or maybe you feel trapped in the status quo. Does the same-old, same-old cloud your every morning? There's a saying that sums up this scenario: *Unless you are moving forward, you are losing ground.*

Anything that stops growing starts dying. There is no true "static state" in life. If water doesn't flow, it stagnates. If a rose doesn't bloom, it wilts. If a muscle doesn't work, it atrophies. Living is all about progressing, moving on, and pressing forward. But you can't see the road ahead if you are constantly looking over your shoulder at where you have been—sooner or later you will end up in a ditch. For many of us, our biggest problem with moving into the future is that *we are stuck in the past.*

Believe me, *everyone* has some sort of skeleton in the closet. We all have things in our past that we would rather forget. We all have made mistakes. Each of us has done things we wish we could undo and said things we wish we could unsay. None of us is perfect.

1

"You can't see the road ahead if you are constantly looking over your shoulder at where you have been— sooner or later you will end up in a ditch."

Our pasts are all different and some are better than others. You may have a past that brings such a heavy weight of guilt and condemnation into your life that you cannot even *see* your future. If you are like me, you have had times when you feel like you are the only one who has failed God. To one degree or another, we all have pasts that we wish we could change.

Unfortunately, that is not possible. The past is the past; it cannot be changed. Sometimes we simply have to decide to pick up and go on. That's the lesson Simba, the young lion cub, had to learn in Disney's *The Lion King*. When Simba met Pumbaa the warthog and Timon the meerkat, he was advised by them to put his past behind him. Or, in Pumbaa's words, "You've got to put your behind in your past." Either way, Simba couldn't change what had happened; he could only go on.

There is nothing you can do about your past either. But, even though you cannot change where you have been, you *can* change where you are going. Your past may haunt you, but in Christ you also have a bright future ahead. You may have fallen short of the glory of God, but He does not want you to stay there. With God's help, you can put your past behind you and step into the glorious future that He desires for you.

Even as born-again followers of Christ, our past has a way of tagging along behind us, nagging at us and forcing us to spend a lot of time struggling with unresolved issues. Perhaps you still hurt from a messy divorce. Maybe your emotions are crippled from growing up in an abusive environment. You could be struggling every day with

2

the anger, shame, regret, and self-hatred that has come from being molested or raped. A sexually immoral past might be haunting you. Perhaps the regret you feel over the time you spent in prison is holding you back from pursuing your dreams. Even now as a Christian, do you sometimes wonder if you can ever overcome the effects and consequences of your past?

I have good news for you. *No matter where you have been or what you have done, you* **can** *overcome your past.* God loves you and wants to help you put your past behind you once and for all. He wants to plunge your past under the blood of Jesus and get rid of it so you can walk in your true destiny. It's time to turn the tables on your past. Instead of letting it stop you, use it to start your future!

Some people fixate on their failures so much that they freeze up and never get beyond them. Focusing so hard on what *was*, they lose all sight of what *can be.* Defeated, disillusioned, and discouraged, they allow their negative past to rob them of a positive future. Knocked down by life, they decide it is useless to try anymore, and they never get back up.

I once heard success described as standing up one time more than you are knocked down. How many people have given up in despair, never knowing how close they were to victory? Where you have been does not have to determine where you go. Just because you have failed in the past does not mean you will fail in the future. Your past mistakes do not control your future destiny. You cannot change your past, but you *can* change your future. God's desire is for you to walk in victory, but first you must learn how to put your past behind you. As Pumbaa told Simba, "You've got to put your behind in your past." If you have got your *behind* in your *past*, it means you are facing *forward*, which is just where you should be. The past is the past, and you must learn to keep it there.

As difficult and painful as it may be to overcome the issues of your past and move forward, it is even more painful to remain stuck in the past. So often we tend to live in the past. We remember the "good old days" *before* our failures and wish things could be the way they used to be. However, as long as we are stuck in the past we will never have much of a future.

Rather than mourning your failures and rehashing your bad memories, learn to regard your past as a learning experience. After all, the very fact that you are still here proves that you have survived. Your past, whether good or bad, has made you stronger and wiser than before. You can take the lessons you learned and walk forward in victory. And as a survivor, you can help other people with backgrounds similar to your own to survive and become victors as well.

> *"Where you have been does not have to determine where you go."*

We can take advantage of our mistakes by learning from them. While living a carefree lifestyle with his friends Pumbaa and Timon, the day came when Simba's past rose up and confronted him. A decision faced the young lion: Should he stay where he was or return home to claim his destiny as king?

Speaking to Rafiki, a baboon who served as a spiritual guide in the story, Simba said, "I know what I have to do, but going back means I'll have to face my past. I've been running from it for so long."

At that point Rafiki promptly rapped Simba on the head with his wooden staff. When the lion protested, "What was that for?" Rafiki replied, "It doesn't matter. It's in the past."

"Yeah, but it still hurts," said Simba.

Rafiki answered, "Oh yes, the past can hurt, but the way I see it, you can either run from it or learn from it." Then he illustrated his point—the monkey took another swipe at Simba with his staff, and the lion promptly ducked. He had learned from the past!

Hopefully, it won't take a smack on the head before you make up your mind! Like Simba, you can choose your future—to go forward to take your place as king or to stay stuck in the place your past has put you.

This is your day and your hour. You have been hurting long enough. You have been down long enough. You have been crushed by guilt and condemnation long enough. It is time to let go of your past and let God do a new thing in your life. He is the God of new beginnings. He has a plan for you and has your best welfare at heart: " 'For I know the plans that I have for you,' declares the LORD, 'plans for welfare and not for calamity to give you a future and a hope' " (Jeremiah 29:11). It is time to quit crying over your past and move into your future. Forget those things that lie behind and reach forward to those things that lie ahead. It is time to make plans for a new beginning and a fresh start.

The Mire of Regret

Before we can put our past behind us, we need to recognize the thoughts, feelings, or attitudes that are keeping us stuck there. One of the strongest of these is *regret*. Perhaps we went somewhere we later wish we had not gone and did things we wish we had not done. Our minds constantly rehearse the "if only" chorus: "If only I hadn't gone to that bar...." "If only I hadn't lost my temper...." "If only I had taken that job...." "If only I hadn't quit school...." "If only...if only...if only..."

Regret can keep you firmly stuck in the past. All it takes is one mistake, and it can affect your entire life. One mistake can leave you bruised, scarred, hurting, and down on yourself for years to come. A single moral lapse or error in judgment can cost you everything: your family, your financial stability, your health, your job, your self-confidence, and your reputation. It could even possibly put you in jail.

If you are mired in regret, you may feel that you have messed up so badly that no one, not even God, can ever forgive you or give you another chance. Sometimes that does happen with human relationships. If you hurt someone or let someone down or betray someone's trust, that person may be unwilling to forgive or trust you again.

God, however, is not that way. He knows all about you and loves you anyway. No matter what you have done, He is not mad at you. Rather, He wants to restore you. The Word of God tells us clearly that, *"If we confess our sins, He is faithful and righteous to forgive us our sins and to cleanse us from all unrighteousness"* (1 John 1:9).

Regret can stop the clock in your life and keep you living in the past. As long as you continually blame yourself for your past mistakes and bad decisions, you will never be able to get ahead. If you

5

cannot learn to accept what happened and move on, all you will do is spin your wheels.

In the Book of Isaiah God said, *"Do not call to mind the former things, or ponder things of the past. Behold, I will do something new"* (Isaiah 43:18–19). Here God is telling us to stop dwelling on our failures, our mistakes, and anything else that has gone before because those things can become a trap for us. Even our past successes can become a hindrance if they tempt us to "rest on our laurels." We need to keep moving. If we are not pressing forward, we are falling back. If we are not growing, we are dying. If we settle for pitching our camp in the wilderness of the past, we will never enjoy the abundant and fertile soil of the future God has planned for us. We cannot afford to let regret hold us back. We need to continually press toward our destiny.

Satan will use your past to try to steal your future. He will throw your failures and mistakes in your face and try to convince you that you have nowhere to go. God, on the other hand, wants you to burn your bridges behind you. As far as He is concerned the past is a closed issue; there is no turning back.

When the children of Israel left Egypt after four hundred years of slavery, their past, in the form of Pharaoh and his army, kept chasing them, trying to draw them back. God showed them that they had to face their past and that, when they did, He would destroy it forever.

So Moses stretched out his hand over the sea, and the sea returned to its normal state at daybreak, while the Egyptians were fleeing right into it; then the LORD overthrew the Egyptians in the midst of the sea. And the waters returned and covered the chariots and the horsemen, even Pharaoh's entire army that had gone into the sea after them; not even one of them remained (Exodus 14:27–28).

There were times when the Israelites regretted leaving Egypt and even talked about trying to return, but God slammed the door and showed them that there was no going back. Don't let regret keep you in the "Egypt" of your past. Move forward into the "promised land" of your full future in Christ.

6

Stuck in the Past

The Mire of Shame

Our natural tendency is to hide the unattractive parts of our lives—particularly our past mistakes and failures. None of us want the skeletons in our closets put on display for the rest of the world to see. *Shame* can keep us mired in the past. Shame causes us to do everything we can to prevent others from finding out what we did, what we were really like, or what happened to us. Whenever someone starts talking about the "good old days," we either leave the room or try to change the subject. Bringing up the past is simply too painful for us.

Perhaps you are unwilling or unable to talk about your past because you are ashamed of it. Do you feel shame today over the baby you had out of wedlock, or the baby you never got to know because you aborted it? Are you so ashamed over your rape or your physical or sexual abuse that you simply can't get past it? Is drug or alcohol addiction the private shame that you are so desperately trying to hide? Did you have an adulterous affair and now are deathly afraid of your spouse finding out? Has sexual promiscuity in your earlier years left you with AIDS or some other kind of sexually transmitted disease, and you are too ashamed to tell anyone?

"As long as you insist on running from your past, you will never get anywhere in life."

While Simba was living the carefree life in the jungle he may have had a lot of fun, but he did not accomplish anything. His life was on hold because he was not fulfilling his destiny. In the same way, as long as you insist on running from your past, you will never get anywhere in life. The more you try to hide your shame, the more havoc it will wreak on your physical, mental, and emotional health. It's time to stop running, confront the shameful parts of your past, and get them under the blood of Jesus so He can destroy them.

This calls for brutal, unblinking honesty on your part. You cannot afford to live in denial any longer. You must look at yourself squarely in the mirror and ask, "Who or what am I running from? What is it I am trying to sweep under the rug? What am I not willing to face?" You need to "'fess up" to your faults and accept full responsibility for your own actions. If your shame is due to someone else's mistreatment of you, you must forgive that person before you can move on. The shame you feel cannot be dealt with until you have forgiven anyone who has hurt you—anyone who stands in need of your forgiveness.

It is only by facing your shameful past that you can be done with it for good. That may not be easy, but it is necessary. Once you stop running and place your past in God's hands, He will nullify it and you can enter a new future with a clean slate. While the Israelites were fleeing Egypt, pursued by Pharaoh and his army, the time came when God told them through Moses to stop running: *"But Moses said to the people, 'Do not fear! Stand by and see the salvation of the* Lord *which He will accomplish for you today; for the Egyptians whom you have seen today, you will never see them again forever. The* Lord *will fight for you while you keep silent' "* (Exodus 14:13–14).

If you will simply stand in the Lord by faith and face this enemy called your past, you will see it swept away before your eyes, along with all the shame, pain, and sorrow associated with it. Like the children of Israel, you must humble yourself under the mighty hand of God, confess your sins, and allow Him to set you free.

In other words, God wants you to leave the past in the past and with confidence turn your heart and mind toward the future. This is exactly what Paul was getting at when he wrote, *"Brethren, I do not regard myself as having laid hold of it yet; but one thing I do: forgetting what lies behind and reaching forward to what lies ahead, I press on toward the goal for the prize of the upward call of God in Christ Jesus"* (Philippians 3:13–14).

Paul was speaking from his own experience of a shameful past. Although he had grown up a devout Jew and Pharisee, Paul's great zeal for God was misguided. Believing he was serving God, Paul had in fact dishonored God by denying Christ and cruelly persecuting those who followed Him. He even became an accomplice to murder in the stoning death of Stephen.

Stuck in the Past

After he became a Christian, Paul certainly must have wrestled frequently with tremendous guilt over his past. At times he must have felt totally unworthy. On the other hand, he also understood that if he was to have any kind of worthwhile future in Christ, he had to get his past behind him once and for all. Even though Paul knew that he could not change what he had done, he also knew that he could be forgiven.

When Paul turned to the Lord in repentance and faith, the blood of Jesus washed away the guilt and shame of his past. Later on he could write, *"I have fought the good fight, I have finished the course, I have kept the faith; in the future there is laid up for me the crown of righteousness, which the Lord, the righteous Judge, will award to me on that day; and not only to me, but also to all who have loved His appearing"* (2 Timothy 4:7–8). What the Lord did for Paul He can do for you.

The Mire of Old Relationships

Another quagmire that can hold you in the past is *old relationships*. Do you still feel drawn romantically to a person from your past, even though that romance is now broken and dead? Do you mourn your lost love and wish things could be the way they once were? Have you found yourself praying that God will bring the two of you back together?

There is a time to stand, but there is also a time to walk away; a time to love, but also a time to leave. The writer of Ecclesiastes said that there is *"a time to search, and a time to give up as lost; a time to keep, and a time to throw away"* (Ecclesiastes 3:6). Sometimes when a relationship is broken you just have to say, "Oh well," chalk it up to experience, and move on. You can't keep putting your life on hold in the hopes that Prince Charming or Sleeping Beauty will reappear out of the mist of the past so you can pick up where you left off. Life rarely works that way. You need to let go, face forward, and press ahead, trusting that the Lord has a brighter future for you than that old relationship you have been longing for.

Some people are continually frustrated over their apparent inability to build fruitful new relationships, unaware that the reason for their failure is that they are stuck in the past. Subconsciously, they compare every new person or circumstance to the ideal of the old that they hold in their memory, and they feel dissatisfied when the new does not measure up.

You have to completely release broken relationships before you can build new ones. You have to let old things die so that new things can come to life. A broken relationship can fracture your ability to trust others, but God wants to help you build a new life. If you place your broken heart under the fountain of Jesus' blood, He will heal your wounds and take away your pain.

Facing Down the Enemy

One reason leaving your past behind can be so difficult is that Satan, your spiritual enemy, will do everything in his power to keep you there. He will throw all your failures back in your face and try to weigh you down with guilt. He will take your knowledge of having failed God and use it to try to convince you that God is mad at you, that He no longer loves you, and that He will not forgive you.

Satan's strategy is to beat you up with guilt and condemnation to the point where you turn away from God and get completely down on yourself. He wants you to believe that you are no good, rotten to the core, and utterly useless to God and everyone else. The message he keeps pounding into your spirit is that you are worthless and without hope because you are such a failure. Sound familiar?

Why should you listen to anything Satan says? The Bible says that the devil is a liar. As a matter of fact, he *invented* lying. Jesus Himself said of Satan, *"He...does not stand in the truth because there is no truth in him. Whenever he speaks a lie, he speaks from his own nature; for he is a liar, and the father of lies"* (John 8:44).

One of Satan's goals is to get you to stop attending church and other kinds of Christian fellowship by so filling you with guilt that you feel unworthy to be around other believers. His plan is to isolate you so he can lie to you. He knows that if he can get you away from the Word of God, he can weaken your ability to counter his lies. If you do not know what God says about your situation, you are much more likely to believe what Satan says.

Stuck in the Past

Remember, *the devil is a liar.* It is time to stand up in the power of the Lord and face down your enemy. As long as you listen to what Satan says about you, you will play right into his hands. If he can keep you in the dark about who you really are and how God really feels about you, he can keep you from fulfilling your destiny.

The devil will rub your nose in your failures for as long as you allow him to. He will constantly try to convince you that you are beyond God's forgiveness and restoration. That is why knowing and believing the Word of God is so important. God's Word is the antidote to Satan's poisonous lies. Consider just a few examples:

He will again have compassion on us; He will tread our iniquities underfoot. Yes, Thou wilt cast all their sins into the depths of the sea (Micah 7:19).

He has not dealt with us according to our sins, nor rewarded us according to our iniquities. For as high as the heavens are above the earth, so great is His lovingkindness toward those who fear Him. As far as the east is from the west, so far has He removed our transgressions from us (Psalm 103:10–12).

When you were dead in your transgressions and the uncircumcision of your flesh, He made you alive together with Him, having forgiven us all our transgressions, having cancelled out the certificate of debt consisting of decrees against us and which was hostile to us; and He has taken it out of the way, having nailed it to the cross (Colossians 2:13–14).

Once you understand and *believe* that God has forgiven you, you can stand up to the guilt and condemnation the devil throws your way and refuse to receive it. You can tell him in the name of Jesus to leave you alone.

The enemy has you on his hit list because he knows what you are capable of doing and becoming as a child of God. Satan does not care about where you have been, but he does care about where you are going. Before you were saved, the devil did not have to worry about you because you were under his power. Now that you are born again, however, you are a huge threat to him. He knows where you are headed and will do everything he can to stop you dead in your tracks. In fact, *your daily struggles with your past are not really about where you have been but where you are headed.* Your fight today is not really about your past but about your future.

> "Your daily struggles with your past are not really about where you have been but where you are headed."

Guilt condemns you to the past and leaves you there, but the conviction of the Holy Spirit will lead you to repentance and a new beginning. No matter how badly you may have messed up in the past, God's grace is sufficient for you. Satan may attack you and some people may try to punish you or wash their hands of you, but God will never abandon you. As Jeremiah says, God has plans for you, plans for a future and a hope.

You may have failed, but failure does not have to be the end of the story. You may have sinned, but your sin does not mean you are finished. What God is looking for is a repentant heart. If you repent of your sin and lay your failure at the feet of Jesus, His blood will wash you clean and you can rise up to a brand-new beginning.

Don't stay stuck in the past. The devil wants to keep you from reaching your full potential in Christ. Whenever he brings up your past, just tell him, "That's under the blood of Jesus." Whenever he tries to heap guilt and condemnation on you, remind him, "In Christ I am the righteousness of God." Whenever he harps about your past failures, inform him, "My past is over and done with, and I have a new and glorious future in Christ Jesus!"

Chapter Two

DON'T LOOK BACK

Now that you have put your past under the blood of Jesus, now that you are confident you have been forgiven and are resolved to press forward into your future, why, you wonder, are you still dealing with the memories of your past? Why isn't it all taken care of? Why do old thoughts and feelings crop up at the most inopportune times?

Simply put, our minds are like computers. Every thought and every experience of our lives is recorded and permanently stored in our mental database. From birth to death, every sound, every image, every smell, every taste, and every touch is filed away in our subconscious mind. Most of this sensory input is hidden so deep that we do not have ready access to it. Nevertheless, whatever is stored in our subconscious influences how we think and act at the conscious level.

We all have memories of things we are not proud of—rash or hateful things we said to someone, or impulsive or foolish things we did. Our words or actions may have deeply hurt someone we love, caused the breakup of a relationship, or even cost us time in jail. Although such events may have occurred many years ago, their memories still fill us with embarrassment, shame, or sorrow.

Adding to the problem is the fact that Satan has a knack for digging through the files of our subconscious and bringing to mind shameful things from our past that we had forgotten. Think about it. How many times have you been praying or worshiping when a shameful memory suddenly popped into your head? It may be something that happened long ago that you haven't thought about in months or even years. All of a sudden, there it is, and you wonder, "Where did *that* come from?" It is one of the enemy's favorite strategies to use our past against us.

Between the bad recollections that we already carry around with us and the ones that Satan causes us to remember, we can have a real struggle in dealing with our memories of the past. Somehow we must learn to bury the past and move on. We cannot afford to judge our future by those memories. Regardless of how often our spiritual enemy reminds us of our past, we must release those memories to God in order to fully realize our future in Christ Jesus.

What memories from your past still fill you with shame today? Your abortion? That time you cheated on your spouse? The day you stole that money from an employer who trusted you? Cheating on the big final exam your senior year in high school? Being molested by your mother's boyfriend? Getting arrested and losing your license because of drunk driving? Those hateful, terrible things you said to your child, your spouse, or your parents? The time you spent in prison for burglary?

Whatever shameful memories you harbor, you need to learn to release them. Although sometimes the consequences of your past actions may follow you for years, the actions themselves are part of a past that is dead and gone. Let go of the dead things of your past. This does not mean you ignore them, particularly if forgiveness or some kind of restitution is needed. Only you, with the help of the Holy Spirit, can decide that. What it does mean is learning not to let your shameful memories from the past form an impassable barrier that prevents you from attaining a better future.

When a loved one dies, we conduct a funeral, bury the person, process our grief, and move on with life. In the same way, burying the dead things in your past is essential to pressing forward to new and greater things. As long as you continue to treat those dead things as though they are alive, they will continue to influence your thoughts and your actions. You must let the dead things stay buried and focus instead on the things that give life.

> *"Let go of the dead things of your past."*

As a believer, when you first became born again you became a brand-new person; the old was done away with. In his second letter to the Corinthian church, Paul explained the process this way: *"Therefore if anyone is in Christ, he is a new creature; the old things passed away; behold, new things have come"* (2 Corinthians 5:17). Now that you are a new creature in Christ, you need to live according to the new, not the old, because the old is dead and buried.

Paul also gave some wise counsel to the Roman Christians in this regard. Even though he was speaking specifically about the old life of sin, his words apply equally to our need to forget our shameful past and take up fully our new lives as children of God.

> *What shall we say then? Are we to continue in sin so that grace may increase? May it never be! How shall we who died to sin still live in it? Or do you not know that all of us who have been baptized into Christ Jesus have been baptized into His death? Therefore we have been buried with Him through baptism into death, in order that as Christ was raised from the dead through the glory of the Father, so we too might walk in newness of life....knowing this, that our old self was crucified with Him, that our body of sin might be done away with, that we should no longer be slaves to sin; for he who has died is freed from sin....Even so consider yourselves to be dead to sin, but alive to God in Christ Jesus* (Romans 6:1–4, 6–7, 11).

It makes no sense to allow dead things to control your life. The time has come for you to leave your past in the past and step forward into your new and living future.

Look to the Future

One of the great principles of the kingdom of God is that once God sets you free and delivers you from sin, you are not to look back. Your future is ahead of you, not behind you. Your promised land beckons from the road before you, not the track you have already walked. With confident trust in the Lord, tell yourself, "My best days are still ahead. I will walk by faith, not by sight."

> *"Your future is ahead of you, not behind you."*

The road to the promised land is a faith road, and faith is demonstrated by obedience. As long as you insist on dwelling in the past, as long as you keep saying, "I can't," you are not walking by faith and will never experience the promised land of the abundant life that God wants you to have and that Jesus came to give you. When we live constantly in the past, we disobey the Lord, who told us to move forward and keep our eyes on the prize. Looking back after God has said to go forward is dangerous.

One day Jesus was discussing with His disciples the question of His return. After telling them that His coming would be like lightning and using as an example the sudden destruction of the wicked in Noah's day, Jesus said,

> *On the day that Lot went out from Sodom it rained fire and brimstone from heaven and destroyed them all. It will be just the same on the day that the Son of Man is revealed. On that day, let not the one who is on the housetop and whose goods are in the house go down to take them away; and likewise let not the one who is in the field turn back. Remember Lot's wife* (Luke 17:29–32).

Jesus' reference to Lot's wife was a warning against looking back instead of moving forward in obedience to God's command. When God resolved to destroy the people of Sodom and Gomorrah because of their wickedness, He sent two angels into Sodom to rescue Lot, who was Abraham's nephew, and his family from the coming destruction.

16

Don't Look Back

Bringing them outside the city, the angels warned them, *"Escape for your life! Do not look behind you, and do not stay anywhere in the valley; escape to the mountains, lest you be swept away"* (Genesis 19:17).

After Lot and his family fled, God rained fire and brimstone on the evil cities. Lot's wife, however, had trouble leaving her past in the past: *"But his wife, from behind him, looked back; and she became a pillar of salt"* (Genesis 19:26). The Lord had delivered her from sin and destruction, but in the end she could not let go of the past and paid for it with her life.

No matter how much you might wish to alter your past, there is no going back. You cannot change where you have been or what you have done. What you *can* do is resolve right now that from this moment forward you will change the direction of your life and your future. That change will be possible only when you agree to let go of the memories of the past, determine not to revisit them, and resolve to look squarely at the road ahead of you. Death and destruction lie in the past, but your future in Christ promises life and abundance.

Memories of past failures or losses can make us afraid to face the future. Unless we give both our memories and fears to the Lord, we will be destined to live our lives in the past. If we allow fear to control us, we will make the wrong decision every time. Whether it is the death of a spouse or a child, a failed marriage or another broken relationship, addiction, abuse, moral failure, or whatever, we all have memories of the past that we need to release today or we cannot move forward.

Anytime we lose something or someone we love, it is hard to understand why. If we dwell on the loss too long the memory will haunt us and affect everything else we try to do. There are some things that we will never figure out no matter how hard we try. That is when we have to simply put them in God's hands and by faith *walk away!*

Are you grieving over losses that you can't seem to let go of? Stop brooding over what might have been. Turn your grief over to the Lord and ask Him to take it. Look your past square in the face and declare, "I'm through with you. You're not going to hold me back anymore! In Jesus' name I am getting up from here and moving on with my life!"

Start a New Chapter

God is looking for people who have repentant hearts. The key to forgetting is being determined to reach forward and press toward the future. Like Paul, we need to forget what is behind us, reach out to what is before us, and *"press on toward the goal for the prize of the upward call of God in Christ Jesus"* (Philippians 3:14).

> *"The key to forgetting is being determined to reach forward and press toward the future."*

If you want to forget the past, then accept the fact that your past is something you simply cannot change. It is a waste of time to try. Break the cycle. Stop calling your friends on the phone to rehash old issues. Stop wishing that you could turn the clock back. Don't waste time dwelling on the memories of a lost love or a broken heart. Quit talking about the past and make new plans for the future. There is no better time than today to get your painful, shameful, and crippling memories behind you.

Wouldn't it be sad to come to the end of your life only to discover that you had wasted it because of living in the past? As a believer, you are a new creature in Christ. You have too much living to do to waste your time being weighed down by your past and haunted by its memories. You cannot afford to give up because a new day of victory, prosperity, and abundance is at hand. In Christ, your success is closer than you imagine.

Stop blaming yourself constantly for your mistakes and torturing yourself with the memories of your failures. Instead, confess them before the Lord, receive His forgiveness, and walk by faith into the future He has prepared for you. Stop revisiting the old failed schemes of the past and grab hold of God's new plans for your life.

What memories are you hanging on to? Let go of them. Make up your mind that what's done is done. Close this chapter of your life and let God write a new one. He wants you to close the book on your past memories once and for all. Turn your memories over to Him and trust Him to take care of them. He will lift a weighty burden from your shoulders. Armed with a new sense of strength and freedom you will be able to fix your eyes forward, step out briskly, and proclaim boldly to the world, "My best days are still ahead!"

Cleansed by the Blood

The most effective way to deal with shameful and painful memories is to place them under the blood of Jesus. The Bible calls Jesus the *"Lamb of God who takes away the sin of the world"* (John 1:29). He shed His blood as our Passover Lamb so that we could get our past behind us and begin again in Him as new creatures. Because of His sacrifice and death on the cross, we can call on the name of Jesus and His blood will wash us clean of all the sin, guilt, and baggage of our past.

None of us are perfect; as we go through life we inevitably will make mistakes. We will fall into sin. At times we will do things that we will regret and that will leave us hurting, and perhaps others as well. Whenever that happens, we must repent, or turn from our sin, go to the Lord, apply His blood for our cleansing, and move on.

There have been times in my own life when I thought that my failures were too bad for God to forgive. By His grace, however, I learned that the blood of Jesus is more powerful than any of the sins or failures of my past.

The same is true for you. No matter what you have done, no matter how horrible your past or how shameful your memories, there is nothing in your life—past, present, or future—that is beyond the cleansing power of the blood of Jesus. Ask yourself the questions posed in the old gospel hymn, "Have you been to Jesus for the cleansing power? Are you washed in the blood of the Lamb?" Hebrews 9:14 says that the *"blood of Christ"* cleanses our conscience *"from dead works to serve the living God."* That is your choice: Either you are serving the dead works of the past or you are serving the living God as a new creature in Christ.

Our memories, good or bad, can hold us in the past. Bad memories are a form of bondage that chains us to old situations we should have forgotten long ago. Good memories can cause us to long for the old days or to become too easily satisfied with where we are. Both kinds of memories can blind us to the future and keep us from moving forward.

Have you ever felt so badly about your past that all you could do was constantly berate and punish yourself over it? Do you remember how depressed you became when nothing you did could take away the guilt or shame or pain you felt? Here is some *good* news: Jesus took your punishment upon Himself two thousand years ago so that you could go free! Romans 8:1 says, *"There is therefore now no condemnation for those who are in Christ Jesus."*

As a believer, you do not need to punish yourself, because Jesus took your punishment. It no longer applies to you. You can let go of the past and its memories that haunt you and let the blood of Jesus take them away. This does not mean you will develop amnesia. You may still remember the past, but through Jesus' blood the pain of those memories will be gone.

Do not fear exhausting God's ability or willingness to cleanse you. His grace is sufficient for all our need—yours, mine, and everyone else's. In the Book of Lamentations, the prophet Jeremiah writes, *"The Lord's lovingkindnesses indeed never cease, for His compassions never fail. They are new every morning; great is Thy faithfulness"* (Lamentations 3:22–23).

God's love for you is eternal and the blood of Jesus is infinitely powerful for cleansing sin. Through Jesus' blood, you can put your sinful past with all its shameful memories behind you once and for all. Instead of constantly rehashing your painful memories, go to the Lord for cleansing.

There is power in the blood of Jesus. There is life in the blood of Jesus. We need power and we need life. Sin has contaminated our human bloodline. We need a *blood transfusion.*

Chapter Three

A BLOOD TRANSFUSION

❦

From earliest times, mankind has recognized the link between blood and life. Ever since Cain murdered his brother Abel and the earth *"opened its mouth to receive* [Abel's] *blood from* [Cain's] *hand"* (Genesis 4:11), man has understood that human life is inseparably bound to blood. At the same time, blood has significance in the spiritual realm as well. In a way that we cannot completely comprehend, the shedding of blood is a critical factor in our salvation as Christians. Leviticus 17:11 says, *"For the life of the flesh is in the blood, and I have given it to you on the altar to make atonement for your souls; for it is the blood by reason of the life that makes atonement."* Life is in the blood.

Without blood there is no life, for the flesh gets its life from the blood. Anytime a person suffers a serious bleeding injury, surgeons have to make sure they reattach any severed blood vessels so that the tissues continue to have adequate blood supply. Without blood, the tissues will die.

Blood is a very unique substance. While the human body contains many liquid compounds, blood is actually living tissue. Where there is no blood, the flesh dies. Have you ever wrapped a rubber band or tied a piece of string tightly around your finger? What happens? After only a few minutes your finger turns blue and becomes numb because it is not getting sufficient blood supply. Cut the blood off long enough, and your finger will eventually die and fall off. The life of the flesh is in the blood.

God created man from the dust of the earth and then breathed into him the breath of life. Oxygen goes directly into our bloodstream by way of the lungs. It is an amazing process where oxygen diffuses through the walls of the lungs into the blood, and waste gases pass from the blood to the lungs and are expelled when we exhale. Life is in the blood.

Our human blood sustains the life of our physical bodies. The blood of Jesus provides spiritual life. His blood possesses resurrection power: *"Now the God of peace, who brought up from the dead the great Shepherd of the sheep through the blood of the eternal covenant, even Jesus our Lord"* (Hebrews 13:20). In other words, God used Jesus' own blood—the *"blood of the eternal covenant"*—to raise Him from the dead.

In Moses' day, the tabernacle was the place where the blood of animal sacrifices was offered to atone for the sins of the people. The ninth chapter of Hebrews reveals that Israel's earthly tabernacle was merely a model of a greater heavenly tabernacle:

> But when Christ appeared as a high priest of the good things to come, He entered through the greater and more perfect tabernacle, not made with hands, that is to say, not of this creation; and not through the blood of goats and calves, but through His own blood, He entered the holy place once for all, having obtained eternal redemption...And according to the Law, one may almost say, all things are cleansed with blood, and without shedding of blood there is no forgiveness (Hebrews 9:11–12, 22).

In the earthly tabernacle, the high priest would go into the Holy of Holies once a year and apply the blood of the sacrifice to the mercy seat over the ark of the covenant. If the high priest entered the

A Blood Transfusion

Holy of Holies without perfect blood, he would die. No one could stand before God without the blood!

Jesus came to earth so He could give His perfect blood to wash us clean of our sin once and for all. No longer would we need the blood of unblemished animals to symbolize the covering of our sin. The blood of Jesus brought genuine cleansing. When Jesus died, He descended into the earth and was raised from the dead three days later. He then ascended into heaven, entered the heavenly tabernacle, and applied His blood to the mercy seat. Jesus' blood possesses true power to cover our sin and cleanse us from it forever.

"Life is in the blood."

The blood of Jesus Christ was not just any blood; it was the blood of God. His blood was *perfect* blood, untainted by the sinfulness of mankind. Jesus was born to a virgin named Mary. He was conceived in her womb by the Holy Spirit. This means that Jesus had no earthly or biological father.

During pregnancy, a mother does not share her blood with the baby in her womb. Babies develop their own blood supply that does not come from the mother. Although the mother provides nutrients that the baby receives through the umbilical cord, the mother's blood never passes beyond the placenta, the membrane that separates her from her growing baby. The mother's blood is on one side of the placenta while the baby's is on the other. The baby's blood does not mix with the mother's blood. In fact, many times a baby's blood type is different from the mother's blood type.

This is important when we consider the birth of Jesus. Since He had no biological father, and since He shared no blood with His mother, Jesus' blood could have come only from heaven. Even though she was His mother, Mary did not determine Jesus' blood. His blood came from the Father through the Holy Spirit. Jesus received a physical body through Mary, but His blood came from heaven rather than from man. His body was like ours, but His blood was not contaminated like ours. Jesus had perfect blood.

Contaminated Blood

All of us as humans share a common blood disorder. We have contaminated blood. It is a universal condition. When Adam and Eve disobeyed God, their sin infected their blood, and they passed their condition on to every succeeding generation. Every one of us is infected.

Sin is in our blood. No one has to teach us to do wrong; it comes naturally. We don't have to teach our children to lie. They will lie as soon as they can talk. Just as we did, our children will learn to sin on their own without our help. It's in their blood. Sin is a spiritual disease passed down to us by our ancestors, and by us to our children. They, in turn, will pass it to their children. Because of the sin of Adam and Eve, the entire human race has been infected in the blood.

Cain murdered his brother because sin was in his blood. As humans we hate and oppress and abuse one another and go to war against one another because sin is in our blood. Every one of us has a sin nature, and it is that sin nature that drives us to destruction. It may lie dormant for a little while, but it always comes out eventually.

Consider the story of the South Carolina mother who is now serving a life sentence for murdering her children. One day she strapped her two toddlers into their car seats, released the brake, and let the car roll into a lake, drowning her sons. To this day she does not know why she did it. In Texas, another mother was convicted of drowning her five children in the bathtub. She, too, does not know why she did it. In both cases, abuse and depression likely played a part, but in the end it still comes down to sin in the blood.

Our prisons are overflowing and our psychiatric wards are full. Drugs, alcohol, and violent crime plague our streets. Suicide is almost epidemic in proportion. Adultery, homosexuality, and other sexual sins are commonplace. Abortion continues to be a scourge on the land. The institutions of marriage and the family are under increasing attack.

Faced with all these things, we may feel like wringing our hands and crying, "What are we going to do?" So-called "experts" offer theories and the government spends dollars by the millions, but the problems only get worse. AIDS is not the problem. Environment is not the problem. Education is not the problem. Troubled neighborhoods are not the problem. Insufficient funding of social programs is not the problem. *Sin is the problem.* It's in our blood.

We can build all the prisons we like. We can devise all the social programs we want and spend millions of dollars on them. None of it will work. Until the blood of Jesus touches our hearts and changes us from the inside out, we will never change. Without the blood of Jesus to cure our blood infection, we are destined to destroy ourselves and each other. We need a blood transfusion!

Hope for all mankind comes through the blood of Jesus Christ. Our salvation comes through His blood. So does our healing. Jesus' blood brings us deliverance. Wholeness and immortality are ours through the blood of Jesus. His blood is perfect blood. His blood is uncontaminated blood. The blood of Jesus has the

> ## *"Sin is the problem. It's in our blood."*

power to wash away sin, heal the sick, and raise the dead. Our blood will only bring us death. In Jesus' blood we find life!

The Jews of Jesus' day were horrified when He said, *"Unless you eat the flesh of the Son of Man and drink His blood, you have no life in yourselves. He who eats My flesh and drinks My blood has eternal life; and I will raise him up on the last day. For My flesh is true food, and My blood is true drink"* (John 6:53–55). What a statement! No wonder that from that moment on, the Jewish religious leaders were dead set against Jesus and determined to do away with Him! Even many of those who had been following Jesus turned away from Him after He spoke of His flesh and blood in this way.

To them it was as though Jesus was advocating cannibalism, something that was repugnant to them and forbidden by the Law. They failed to recognize that Jesus was speaking figuratively. They did not understand that He carried the divine life of God in His veins. It never occurred to them that they needed to partake of His flesh and blood in a spiritual sense in order to obtain eternal life. There was life in Jesus' blood, but they failed to see it.

A Wonderful Love Story

Isaiah prophesied of the coming Messiah that He would be so disfigured that He would not even resemble a man. Before He was crucified, Jesus was whipped and beaten to a bloody pulp, punished so brutally that any other man might have died from it. That alone might have been enough to disfigure Jesus almost beyond recognition, but I believe there was more at work. Consider Isaiah's words:

Surely our griefs He Himself bore, and our sorrows He carried; yet we ourselves esteemed Him stricken, smitten of God, and afflicted. But He was pierced through for our transgressions, He was crushed for our iniquities; the chastening for our well-being fell upon Him, and by His scourging we are healed (Isaiah 53:4–5).

The prophet says that the Messiah was *"smitten of God."* Certainly, this means that Jesus' crucifixion and all the brutal treatment leading up to it was part of God's purpose for His Son. But it also means that *God Himself* laid on Jesus our griefs and sorrows, our transgressions and iniquities. God the Father *smote* His Son with all of our sin, and it was our sin borne on Jesus' body that so disfigured Him.

Try to imagine how ravaged a body would be that bore the effects of every sin and every sickness known to humanity! Such a body certainly would not look human. Jesus knew no sin or sickness, but He became sin and sickness on the cross for us. As He bore those things in His body, they made Him so ugly that He did not even resemble a man. Yes, Jesus was brutally beaten and abused, but it was sin that truly made Him ugly.

Until He hung on the cross, Jesus had known no sin or evil. As their crushing weight bore down on His shoulders, we can understand why He cried out, *"My God, My God, why hast Thou forsaken Me?"* (Matthew 27:46) At that moment, Jesus tasted sin and evil for the very first time.

When was the last time you really thought about what Jesus did for you? He became sin so you could be saved. He became sickness so you could be healed. He was cursed so you could be blessed. He tasted evil so you could taste holiness. The wages of sin is death, and sin always pays its due. Jesus paid the price for your sin so you could go free. Sin brings hurt, sorrow, and destruction in its wake, yet Jesus bore it gladly for you. He willingly endured the disfigurement of sin so you could be made whole, without spot or blemish. He did all of this because He loves you. What a wonderful love story!

The Romans did not kill Jesus; neither did the Jews. It was *God* who afflicted Him for our sake, for our sin: *"All of us like sheep have gone astray, each of us has turned to his own way; but the LORD has caused the iniquity of us all to fall on Him"* (Isaiah 53:6). Jesus was so full of God's life that nobody could kill Him. He said, *"I lay down My life so that I may take it again"* (John 10:17). When the time came for Jesus to die, He said, *"It is finished,"* then bowed His head and gave up His spirit. No one took Jesus' life. He gave it up freely and willingly.

> *"When was the last time you really thought about what Jesus did for you?"*

Jesus had to surrender His life because otherwise death could not have touched Him. How could the Creator and Source of life be subject to death? There is no way that humanity could ever have killed the Lord of glory. The Creator of heaven and earth had to lay aside all His majesty to come to this earth as a lowly man and die in our place. If He was to save us, His divine, life-giving blood had to become contaminated with our sin. In order to die, He had to receive in His blood the nature of death. He had to be cursed, becoming sin for us, so we could become the righteousness of God. He did it of His own free will. What a wonderful love story!

The Power of His Blood

Jesus had such life in His blood that sin could not overpower Him. Sickness could not afflict Him. Death could not touch Him. When Jesus touched death, however, it had to flee. Just ask Lazarus!

(See John 11:1–44.) Just ask the young man and his mother from the village of Nain! (See Luke 7:11–15.) Because of the divine power of God in His blood, Jesus' touch brought life, healing, and wholeness. At His touch, lepers *had* to be healed; the blind *had* to receive their sight; the crippled *had* to walk. All the sick who in faith turned to Jesus for help were made whole by His touch.

Jesus never sinned because His blood was not polluted like ours. His blood was not the blood of man but the blood of God. He achieved complete victory over His flesh because His blood had the life of God in it. We fail to overcome our flesh because our blood is corrupted by sin. That is why we need a transfusion of Jesus' blood. That is why we need to confess Him as Lord with our own mouths, ask His forgiveness, and surrender everything to Him. Only by His blood can we be free and whole.

> *"We need a transfusion of Jesus' blood."*

Human blood is easily contaminated. Once human blood comes into contact with the air, it decomposes rapidly. Before long it starts to stink. Because sin has corrupted it, our human blood is very susceptible to germs and disease.

The blood of Jesus is incorruptible. If you will exercise your faith, you will find that there is enough power in the blood of Jesus to enable you to get all of your past behind you. No matter what happened, no matter what you did or who you did it with, you can put it all behind you through the blood of Jesus. His blood has the power to heal and restore you completely.

Your spiritual enemy does not want you to know about the power of the blood of Jesus. As long as the devil can keep you in the dark about what Jesus' blood has done for you, he can control you. The Bible says that Satan is the accuser of the brethren. He is always ready to jump on your back as soon as you make a mistake and pound you into the ground over it. You will hear his voice inside your head: "Look what you did! You call yourself a Christian? You're nothing but a no-good failure who will never amount to anything! God can't use a loser like you. Besides, He's really mad at you because of what you did. You'd better watch out!"

Don't believe a word of it! Sure, maybe you did mess up, but the blood of Jesus is more powerful than any mistake you have ever made or ever will make. Although it is true that the devil is the accuser of the brethren, the Bible also says that the brethren *"overcame him because of the blood of the Lamb and because of the word of their testimony"* (Revelation 12:11). A testimony is a witness; you testify to what you have seen, heard, or experienced. If the blood of Jesus has touched you and changed you, your testimony combined with His blood can defeat whatever lies the devil throws your way.

When the accuser's voice rises up inside you, take your stand on the blood of Jesus and say, "Wait a minute. Jesus' blood has cleansed me and washed me clean. Devil, you're a liar! The blood of Jesus is on my side! Yes, I failed, but I confessed my sin and Jesus' blood has overcome my past."

The blood of Jesus is more powerful than your past, my past, or anybody's past. I continually praise God for the blood of Jesus that cries out for mercy on my behalf! I don't deserve His mercy, but He has given it to me anyway. God's mercy touches you as well. When you confess your sins and ask the Lord to forgive you, He casts your sins into the sea of forgetfulness and remembers them no longer. If God doesn't remember your sins, why keep bringing them up? Why continue letting the devil beat you up over things the Lord has forgiven and forgotten?

There is power in the blood of Jesus. Jesus poured out His blood so we could have eternal life. He was beaten and whipped, and the divine blood of God flowed. A crown of thorns was crushed down on His head, and His blood fell. Cruel spikes were driven through His hands and feet and He was suspended from a rough wooden cross, and His blood streamed down. His side was pierced by a Roman spear, and His blood poured out.

At the time of the evening sacrifice in the temple, the Lamb of God hanging on an old rugged cross poured out His blood for the sake of lost humanity. He gave His blood so we could receive a blood transfusion. Jesus willingly surrendered His divine blood, becoming sin for us so that we could become the righteousness of God.

The blood of Jesus can do for us what we could never do for ourselves. His blood has the power to cleanse our sins. It has the power to save us. It has the power to heal us. It has the power to make us completely whole. Jesus' blood has the power to make us holy and righteous, without spot or blemish.

As children of God, we have been grafted into His kingdom. Once we were dry branches, dead in our trespasses and sins and cut off from God. Now, through the blood of Jesus, we have been grafted in again. When you want to graft two plants together, you cut a hole in the side of one plant, then take a branch from the other plant and tie it to the first plant at the place where you made the hole. Eventually the grafted branch will grow into and become part of the first plant.

After Jesus died and did away with the old covenant, a soldier pierced His side with a spear, making a hole from which His blood flowed. Through the wound in Jesus' side, each of us who has trusted Christ has been grafted into God's kingdom. Our past is dead and gone and we are now part of the family of God.

God loved us so much that He cut a hole in the side of His Son so we could be brought into His family. By plunging under the blood of Jesus, we have passed from death into life. Jesus has saved us and His life-giving blood flows in our veins. His blood is powerful enough to give everyone on earth a life-saving transfusion.

The blood of Jesus has given you light and life and the power to overcome your past, no matter how bad it is. It has brought you not into religion, but into a living relationship with God through the risen Christ! That relationship makes it possible for you to put behind you all the elements of your past: the regret, the memories, the shame, and most of all, the *guilt*.

Chapter Four

OVERCOMING THE GUILT
OF THE PAST

If you are a born-again believer and follower of Christ, then whether
you realize it or not, *your best days are still ahead of you!* God our
Father has a glorious future in store for all His children, and His purpose will not be defeated. All who truly know Christ have a secure
place in the kingdom of God. Philippians 1:6 says, *"He who began a
good work in you will perfect it until the day of Christ Jesus."* This
means that God will carry the work of salvation, which He began in
you when you trusted Christ, to completion. With confidence in the
promises of God, you should be able to affirm along with Paul that, *"I
know whom I have believed and I am convinced that He is able to
guard what I have entrusted to Him until that day"* (2 Timothy 1:12).

Although many believers would understand the phrase "best
days" as referring primarily to heaven, it means more than that.
Heaven is certainly a wonderful hope and promise, but God wants us
to experience an abundant life *right now.* He wants our future life on
earth to be better than our past. Releasing our past with all its regret,

shame, and bad memories to the Lord and walking by faith does not mean we will never again have to deal with temptation or struggle with the enemy. It *does* mean that as we trust Christ in day-to-day life He will fulfill His purpose in us and lead us into a life of fulfilled potential and spiritual victory.

Even when we know we have been washed in the blood of Jesus and that His blood has overcome our past, we will still face challenges in moving ahead. The devil won't give up without a fight. One of the biggest struggles many believers face comes in confronting their *guilt* over their past. How about you? Does guilt about your past hang over you like a dark cloud that never goes away? Have you tried and tried, but simply cannot let go of it? If so, you are not alone.

Dealing with guilt is a universal human experience. Guilt causes more emotional and psychological problems and puts more people in mental institutions than any other single issue. Unresolved guilt can devastate our lives and even kill us. Even more than regret, shame, or bad memories, guilt can stop us cold and sabotage any chance at a better life.

Guilt is the emotional and mental state of a person who has committed an offense of some kind, especially when that offense is conscious and deliberate. Such a person stands deserving of judgment and punishment. We know when we are guilty of something because our conscience accuses us. Over and over in our minds a persistent inner voice tells us, "You know what you did was wrong. You ought to be punished."

Genuine guilt is bad enough—all of us have plenty of *that* to deal with—but adding to the problem is the fact that we also may carry around a lot of *false* guilt. False guilt is a form of self-reproach where we feel inadequate or personally responsible for offenses that exist only in our minds. In other words, we blame ourselves needlessly for offenses that never occurred.

It is sometimes hard to tell the difference between genuine and false guilt. Either way, their effects are the same. Both are equally dangerous to your mental, emotional, spiritual, and even physical health. Learning to overcome the guilt of your past, genuine or not, is one of the most important keys to growing spiritually and to making the days ahead your "best days."

Overcoming the Guilt of the Past

Dealing With the Spirit of Failure

Whenever we sin as believers, something inside us lets us know that we deserve to be punished. Working in conjunction with our conscience, the voice of the Holy Spirit convicts us of our sin. The Spirit, however, also reminds us of what Jesus did for us. Once we know by faith that Jesus took our punishment on the cross, we realize that we do not have to beat ourselves up over the things we've done wrong. If, however, we allow guilt to fester in our lives long enough, we will end up depressed and ashamed, and we will walk under a false spirit of failure. So until we deal with our guilt, we will never experience the full joy and abundant life that God wants us to have.

As humans, we all share a common sin-guilt before God: *"For all have sinned and fall short of the glory of God"* (Romans 3:23). At one time we all were *"dead in* [our] *trespasses and sins"* (Ephesians 2:1), *"but God, being rich in mercy, because of His great love with which He loved us, even when we were dead in our transgressions, made us alive together with Christ (by grace you have been saved), and raised us up with Him, and seated us with Him in the heavenly places in Christ Jesus"* (Ephesians 2:4–6).

In Christ our guilt is gone, but it is not always easy for us to just let it go. Satan always stands ready to accuse us. Revelation 12:10 describes Satan as the accuser of the brethren who accuses them before God day and night. In fact, the name *Satan* literally means "accuser." If we are born again, Satan will constantly accuse us of all our failures. His objective is to so weigh us down with guilt that we will live under a spirit of failure all our lives.

Do you feel like a loser? Have you failed in school? Your career? Your marriage? Are you convinced that anything you attempt is doomed to failure from the start? Does it seem pointless even to try? Have you started to agree with people who say that you are hopeless and will never make anything of yourself? Have you accepted the label, "No Good," that they have attached to you?

Feelings like these may indicate that you are living under a spirit of failure. There is a difference between failing and being a failure. Everybody fails at one time or another. Just because you failed in the past does not mean you have to continue to fail. A spirit of failure will cause you to define your life by your failures rather than by your accomplishments.

People who overcome guilt and failure learn to regard their failures not as liabilities but as stepping-stones to success. Failure does not have to define your life. The difference between being a failure and being an overcomer lies in your ability to learn from your mistakes. A spirit of failure will keep you focused on your inabilities—the things you *cannot* do.

> "There is a difference between failing and being a failure."

If your spiritual enemy can cause you to walk in guilt and self-condemnation, he can sabotage your earthly destiny and rob you of your heavenly rewards. Rewards in heaven are based on faithfulness on earth. Satan cannot keep you out of heaven, but he can distract you with guilt so that you take your eyes off of Jesus. As long as you are pre-occupied with your guilt and failure, you cannot serve the Lord with your whole heart. Rewards you might otherwise have earned you will lose because you allowed the devil to mess with your mind and make you feel guilty for sins that Christ has already forgiven.

That is how Satan can steal your future. If he can cause you to feel bad enough about yourself, your past, and your life in general that you stop walking by faith, he can prevent you from doing greater things for God and from receiving and enjoying all the promises of God.

Notice too that the devil is the accuser of the *brethren*. This means that he attacks and accuses people who love the Lord. Satan is not concerned about unbelievers; they are already securely in his camp. His goal is to accuse Christians of their failures and to try to hold them down spiritually and emotionally.

Satan wants you to believe that you are a failure who is beyond God's ability or willingness to restore. Over and over he will condemn you with thoughts like, "Man, you really blew it! Look how bad you messed up! Some Christian *you* are! Do you really think God

34

still loves you after what you did? It's all over! You may as well hang it up!" If he can clobber you with guilt and make you doubt your salvation, he can hold you in the grip of failure and keep you from moving forward.

Another of the devil's strategies is to tempt you to sin, and when you give in, to throw your sin back in your face as proof of your worthlessness. He will whisper in your ear, "You're no good. God can't use someone like you. If you were *really* saved, you wouldn't have done what you did."

> *"Nothing energizes the human spirit like a clear conscience."*

None of us are perfect, and we all tend to carry around at least some degree of guilt. This makes it easy for us to cave in to the devil's lies. Make up your mind now to pay no attention to what the enemy says. If you listen to his lies long enough, you will start to believe them, and before long you will be beating up on yourself worse than the devil ever did. Any baggage of guilt that you carry around feeds the spirit of failure in your heart, making it difficult, if not impossible, for you to get ahead.

You can overcome your guilt by confessing your sin, turning from your sin, and receiving God's forgiveness. This restores your fellowship with the Lord as well as your ability to walk confidently by faith. Nothing energizes the human spirit like a clear conscience. Remember the promise of 1 John 1:9, that if you confess your sin, the Lord will forgive you and cleanse you of all unrighteousness—not some, but *all.*

Plunge Your Guilt Under the Blood of Jesus

Even when you confess your sin and ask for God's forgiveness, you may still *feel* unforgiven if you allow the devil to create doubt in your mind. This is one reason why it is so important to walk by faith and by the Word of God and not by feelings. Feelings are unreliable; they change according to our circumstances, mood, physical health, and brain chemical levels. The Word of God stands, regardless of our feelings. If you have confessed your sins and asked for God's forgiveness, *He has forgiven you.* That is a fact based on the promise of God's Word and does not depend on the way you feel.

Once you truly understand the truth that you are forgiven, you will be able to speak against any doubts that the devil puts in your mind. We speak either from faith or from disbelief, and the words we say can determine whether or not we overcome the haunting feelings of past guilt and go on to build an intimate relationship with Jesus Christ.

You *can* overcome the guilt of your past. Remember that as a Christian, you have received a blood transfusion where the blood of Jesus gives you the power to defeat your accuser. By plunging your guilt under the blood of Christ, you can be freed from that guilt. Your weapons against the enemy are the blood of the Lamb and the word of your testimony, both of which are founded on the Word of God. Jesus is the Lamb, and He is also the Word (see John 1:1), the very expression of God Himself. Jesus is the Word of God personified. Your testimony is based on God's faithfulness to His Word and to His promises in forgiving you, cleansing you of sin, and saving you.

How exactly does the blood of Jesus overcome our accuser? To understand this we must review the story of Moses and the origin of the Jewish festival of Passover. The Israelites had been slaves in Egypt for four hundred years when God chose Moses to lead them to freedom. Under God's direction, Moses went repeatedly before Pharaoh, demanding that he free the children of Israel. Time after time Pharaoh refused, and each time God sent a plague upon Egypt to convince them of His power. Each time Pharaoh refused, the plagues grew more severe.

Finally, with the last plague, God achieved the release of His people by sending a death angel to kill all the firstborn in the land, both man and animal. In order to spare the Israelites, God instructed them to mark their homes with a special sign. They were to slaughter a lamb, drain its blood into a basin, and, with a branch of hyssop, spread the blood on the lintel and doorposts of the house. When the death angel saw the blood, he would know that this home was "under the blood"—in a covenant relationship with God—and would "pass over" that house and spare everyone inside.

The blood above and on either side of the door was symbolic, a foreshadowing of the cross on which Jesus Christ, the Lamb of God, shed His blood for the sins of the world. All who have been born again by accepting Jesus Christ as their personal Savior and Lord are "under the blood," and God's wrath will pass over them without harm.

In the old covenant, the high priest would sprinkle the blood on the mercy seat in the Holy of Holies in the temple. Once the blood was applied to the mercy seat, the sins of the people were forgiven. All the ceremony and symbolism of the blood on the doorposts and on the mercy seat pointed forward to Christ, the Lamb of God, slain from the foundation of the world.

So what do you do when the weight of guilt from your accuser threatens to crush you? First, confess all sin that you are aware of, trusting the Holy Spirit to reveal any that may be hidden from you. Second, settle in your heart that the blood of Jesus is more powerful than your past. It is more powerful than your sin and guilt. When you confess your sin, you acknowledge your guilt before God, but when you apply the blood of Jesus, you acknowledge the power of the blood to cleanse your sin and remove your guilt.

Left unforgiven, your sin *will* condemn you. Once you place yourself "under the blood," however, you are free from guilt and judgment. Remember Paul's words that *"there is therefore now no condemnation for those who are in Christ Jesus"* (Romans 8:1). Your sin is taken away and can no longer hold you down. The blood of Jesus sets you free to pursue the full destiny that God has for you.

Guilt vs. Conviction

Sometimes believers are confused over the difference between guilt and conviction. *Guilt* is the result of sin and is destructive in nature. Left unresolved, it leads to condemnation. As such, it is one of Satan's favorite and most effective weapons against us. *Conviction* is a work of the Holy Spirit and is redemptive in nature. When we sin, the Holy Spirit convicts us of our sin, not to make us feel bad but to lead us to repent and get it under the blood of Jesus.

Guilt condemns us and tears down our sense of self-worth. It feeds on our shame and makes us inclined to try to avoid God. Conviction draws us toward God and affirms our self-worth while leading us to acknowledge and deal honestly with our sin. Guilt relates to law and judgment; conviction, to grace and mercy.

Jesus did not come to judge the world, but to save it (see John 3:17). Are you saved? Have you confessed all known sin in your life? Have you sought and claimed God's forgiveness on the basis of the blood of Jesus? If you have done these things yet still feel weighed down with guilt, you can be confident that it is not God's judgment pressing you down, but is a result of Satan's effort to condemn you.

Think about a time when you sinned and really let God down. Didn't you feel like kicking yourself for a week in remorse over what you did? There is nothing wrong with that as long as it led you to repent, confess, and get back up to go on, trusting in God's forgiveness and depending on Him to help you do better. That is how the conviction of the Holy Spirit works in our hearts.

When we allow guilt to control our lives we tend to avoid church. We stop seeking out godly friends, we stop reading and studying the Bible, and we stop praying. In short, we abandon the very things that can keep us going and bring us victory. We resort to old bad habits, thought patterns, and lifestyles. Guilt feeds on guilt. The knowledge that we have backslidden from God adds new guilt to that which is already pressing us down, and we end up worse off than before.

As believers, we don't have to live that way. The Lord has given us a way to escape our guilt. God's grace is sufficient for us. If we confess and repent, we are forgiven. Our guilt is lifted—*all of it.* The only guilt we bear is the guilt we refuse to lay down and the guilt we allow Satan to load on our backs. Guilt enslaves us but Christ came to free us. Galatians 5:1 says, *"It was for freedom that Christ set us free; therefore keep standing firm and do not be subject again to a yoke of slavery."*

Even after repenting and confessing, you may not always *feel* forgiven, but that does not matter because you cannot judge by your feelings. This is where the word of your testimony comes into play. In all things you must go by what the Word of God says. You are not forgiven because you *feel* forgiven but because God *said* you are forgiven. God's Word is true; what He said you can say also.

Don't continue living under a cloud of guilt. Jesus took your guilt away completely when He died on the cross. He liberated you from your past so you could press ahead into your future. When the devil tries to lay a guilt trip on you, stand on the Word of God and testify, "I once was guilty, but now I am free! I am forgiven on the basis of the blood of Jesus shed for me and no one can condemn me. I am forgiven and free because God said so!"

> *"Guilt enslaves us but Christ came to free us."*

Repentance Is Essential

Sin always leaves us feeling guilty. God's laws are for our protection, and when we break them, they end up breaking us. However, there is no condemnation for those who are in Christ Jesus (see Romans 8:1). Paul went on to say, *"For the law of the Spirit of life in Christ Jesus has set* [us] *free from the law of sin and of death"* (Romans 8:2). In other words, death comes with sin, but life comes with repentance of sin. *Repentance* means to turn away from sin and turn to God. When we turn away from sin we turn away from death. When we turn to Christ we turn to life because He *is* life.

The Gospels relate the stories of two of Jesus' disciples whose experiences illustrate the importance of repentance. Judas Iscariot betrayed the Lord for thirty pieces of silver. Simon Peter denied three times that he even knew Jesus. Two different men with two different issues, but they both failed. Peter repented of his sin of denial, received forgiveness, and was restored to fellowship with the Lord. He went on to become a courageous and fearless leader and apostle in the early church. Judas failed to repent and ended up killing himself. Both men were guilty of grievous sins. Both men experienced guilt and condemnation. One repented, was forgiven, and went on with God. The other did not, and he died tragically by his own hand.

All Judas had to do was confess his sins, receive forgiveness, and overcome the enemy by the blood of the Lamb and the word of his testimony. He could have been restored and finished his ministry, had he only seen his guilt as a warning sign. Up to the very moment he took his life he could still have repented of his sins and been forgiven and cleansed of all his guilt.

On Resurrection Sunday, as Mary Magdalene, Mary the mother of James, and Salome approached Jesus' tomb, an angel appeared to them and said, *"Do not be amazed; you are looking for Jesus the Nazarene, who has been crucified. He has risen; He is not here; behold, here is the place where they laid Him. But go, tell His disciples and Peter, 'He is going before you into Galilee; there you will see Him, just as He said to you' "* (Mark 16:6–7).

Peter had failed Christ in such a way that he felt he could not go on. Guilt threatened to destroy his future, so God sent an angel to reach out to Peter and to let him know *personally* that God was not mad at him and that everything was going to be all right.

God has the same word for you today. He is not mad at you. No matter what you have done, no matter how much guilt you bear, all is forgiven if you will repent, confess, and turn to Him. His grace is sufficient for you. No sin is too great for the blood of Jesus to wash away. Nothing you have done is beyond His forgiveness. He who with the single word "Forgiven!" can wipe out all of your sin in an instant, is waiting for you to repent. Simply trust Him, and He will work everything out in your life.

Worthy in Christ

The good news of the Gospel is that even if you have made a million mistakes or have failed God more times than you can remember, you can be forgiven. You can put your guilty past behind you and start over. I could not begin to count the number of times I have let God down, yet I keep on repenting and He keeps on forgiving. If God can forgive, restore, and use somebody like me, then He can forgive, restore, and use anyone.

You might protest, "But you don't know how many times I've failed! You don't know the things that I've done! I am too unworthy for God to use!" To that I would reply, "Welcome to the club!" None of us are worthy. We all have failed; we all have made mistakes. *"For all have sinned and fall short of the glory of God"* (Romans 3:23); *"They have all turned aside; together they have become corrupt; there is no one who does good, not even one"* (Psalm 14:3). Yes, in ourselves we are unworthy, but the blood of Jesus turns that around.

The blood of Jesus speaks for us and declares that we are not guilty. His blood *makes* us worthy. Our sins are washed away and we become righteous, not by our own merit, but by the grace and plan of God: *"He made Him who knew no sin to be sin on our behalf, that we might become the righteousness of God in Him"* (2 Corinthians 5:21). *"For all of you who were baptized into Christ have clothed yourselves with Christ"* (Galatians 3:27). Jesus Christ is without sin, absolutely righteous, and eminently worthy. If you have clothed yourself with Christ, His worthiness makes you worthy.

> *"His blood makes us worthy."*

It is vitally important to get this understanding deep into your spirit because as long as you feel unworthy, you will never believe that God truly wants to help you. As long as you feel unworthy, you will never exercise your faith and grow the way God wants you to. As long as you feel unworthy, you will never get beyond your guilt or your failures. As long as you feel unworthy, you will never believe God to get a better house or a better job or a godly husband or wife.

We all have made mistakes and we will continue to make them as long as we live because none of us are perfect. This fact does not change what God has said about us or what the blood of Jesus has done for us. Paul understood this as well as anyone. This great apostle and mighty man of God knew a lot about failure. He wrote:

> For that which I am doing, I do not understand; for I am not practicing what I would like to do, but I am doing the very thing I hate....For I know that nothing good dwells in me, that is, in my flesh; for the wishing is present in me, but the doing of the good is not. For the good that I wish, I do not do;

but I practice the very evil that I do not wish. But if I am doing the very thing I do not wish, I am no longer the one doing it, but sin which dwelleth in me....Wretched man that I am! Who will set me free from the body of this death? Thanks be to God through Jesus Christ our Lord! (Romans 7:15, 18–20, 24–25)

Paul recognized that there is always a struggle in the flesh, especially for believers. He knew that even though someone was born again, the flesh would always try to take over. He also knew that the only path to victory was through the Lord Jesus Christ.

If any believer had to wrestle with guilt, it was Paul. This former archenemy of Christ and His followers learned to put his past behind him through the blood of Christ, and you can too. What was Paul's secret? He learned to *forget* what lay behind him, *reach forward* to what lay before him, and *press toward* the goal of the prize of God's upward call in Christ (see Philippians 3:13–14). The blood of Jesus made this possible for Paul, and it does the same for you.

Like Paul, if you are going to experience success in life, you must get the guilt of your past behind you. Despite how you may feel, you must open your mouth and confess the power that is in the blood of Jesus. The blood of the Lamb and the word of your testimony will overcome the accuser. The arrows of guilt that he fires at you will no longer find a target. With the righteousness of Christ as your armor, and confident in the knowledge that you are forgiven, you can press ahead to all that lies before you in God's good purpose.

Even though you may feel unworthy, the blood of Jesus has covered your yesterday and opened the way to a brighter tomorrow. You don't have to live under a spirit of failure any longer. God never dwells on past failures. He rewards faith and always speaks to us about the future, because the future is where His greatest blessings lie.

Your spiritual enemy will do all he can to deny you the blessings of God. If he can cause you to disobey God's Word, he can stop your blessings. If he can get you to hold on to the past, he can stop your blessings. If he can get you to live in guilt, he can stop your blessings.

Do you feel like you have wrecked your life because of your failures and mistakes? Is guilt over your sins weighing you down so that you can hardly move? Stop wallowing in the guilt of the past. Let the Lord wash away your guilt once and for all. If you diligently obey God and are careful to listen to His Word, He will command His blessings on you, and they will overtake you wherever you go. The spirit of failure will be a thing of the past. You will discover that there is no limit to where you can go, what you can do, or who you can become in the power of Christ.

Your future is wide open! Once you truly know who you are in Christ, you will begin to understand how much God loves you. As you trust in the Lord and grow in Him, your guilt will fall away into the sea of forgetfulness because you will discover the awesome and wonderful truth that *God is not mad at you!*

DON'T JUDGE MY FUTURE BY MY PAST

Chapter Five

GOD IS NOT MAD AT YOU

God is not mad at you. The first time I ever heard that statement was on television from a preacher named T. L. Osborne, and it totally rocked my world. Inside I felt that God *had* to be mad at me because I knew what I'd been doing. Have you ever felt that way? Have you ever had the sneaking suspicion that God was angry with you because you knew you had been messing up and you would be angry if you were in His place? That simple statement, "God is not mad at you," absolutely revolutionized my life. It made me want to know the kind of God who could know everything about me and still not be mad at me.

God is not mad at you. If you allow the truth of that statement to sink deep into your spirit, I predict that it will change your life as radically as it did mine. Not only is God not mad at you, He loves you and has done everything He can to reconcile you to Himself and make you righteous again. Consider Paul's words to the Corinthians:

Therefore if any man is in Christ, he is a new creature; the old things passed away; behold, new things have come. Now all these things are from God, who reconciled us to Himself through Christ, and gave us the ministry of reconciliation, namely, that God was in Christ reconciling the world to Himself, not counting their trespasses against them, and He has committed to us the word of reconciliation. Therefore, we are ambassadors for Christ, as though God were making an appeal through us; we beg you on behalf of Christ, be reconciled to God. He made Him who knew no sin to be sin on our behalf, that we might become the righteousness of God in Him (2 Corinthians 5:17–21).

Paul said that when we turn to Christ in faith and repentance, we become *new creatures.* All the old things have passed away, including our past with all its sin, shame, failure, and guilt. In their place, new things have come. Part of these "new things" should be the awareness that God is not mad at us. The moment we become new creatures in Christ, we enter a process of life changing. As soon as we give our lives to the Lord, He begins to change us. Step by step, from glory to glory, the Spirit of God leads us to grow and mature in Christ.

One of the most significant evidences of our growth is the change in our desires. Growing believers who have become new creatures in Christ no longer desire their old ways of sin. Before I became a Christian, I was afraid to give my life to the Lord because I knew I would have to give up a lot of the things I was doing—things I enjoyed even though they were wrong. Once I did give my life to Christ, however, I discovered that He began changing my desires to conform to His will. As He worked in me, I lost the desire to do all those sinful things I had been afraid to give up.

One thing about God is that He never dwells on the failures of our past. God is not looking for perfect people because He knows there aren't any. He *is* looking for people who will repent; people who will draw nigh unto Him. God is looking for people who will simply love Him. He is looking for people He can bless.

Righteousness and Grace

Since we all have failed God and fallen short of His glory, it is important for us to know who we are in Christ. Paul said that God was reconciling us to Himself through Christ so that in Christ we could become the righteousness of God. We become reconciled to God by confessing and repenting of our sins, asking the Lord to forgive us, and giving our lives to Christ as Savior and Lord. In turn, we become the righteousness of God in Him.

Righteousness means right standing with God. When you give your life to the Lord, God no longer sees you for who you are, but for who Christ has made you to be. Christ covers you with His blood so that God does not see you in your sinfulness. Instead, God sees the

> *"God never dwells on the failures of our past."*

righteousness of His Son covering you, and He considers you right-eous on the basis of that blood covering. You become the righteous-ness of God. You may not always look or act righteous, but the Word of God says that you have become the righteousness of God by the blood of Jesus Christ.

If you want to overcome the failures of your past; if you hope to break the negative patterns, addictions, or obsessive behaviors that control your life, you have to know who you are in Christ. You are no longer the low-down dirty devil dog you used to be. In Christ you are now the righteousness of God. You are *somebody*.

God is not mad at you. Ephesians 2:8 says, *"For by grace you have been saved through faith; and that not of yourselves, it is the gift of God."* Grace is God's undeserved favor, freely given to all who will say, "Jesus, be the Lord of my life." When you receive Jesus as your Lord and Savior, you don't get what you deserve; instead, you get what you need.

Because we all have sinned, we deserve judgment and hell, but we need mercy and forgiveness. God's love for us is so great that when we turn to Christ, He extends His grace so that we receive the mercy we need rather than the judgment we deserve. None of us deserves God's mercy, but He has an endless supply stored up for those who love Him.

People often miss out on God's grace because they feel too unworthy to receive His blessings. Anytime we fail God, our minds tell us, "God is not going to help you." Whenever we mess up, that little voice inside says, "God is going to get you." If we believe that voice, we will shut ourselves off from what God wants to do for us. God is not angry. He loves us and wants to bless us. Grace is not about how good we are, but about how good God is.

Religion or Relationship?

We all have a tendency to believe that if we are good, then God will help us. It's the old "you scratch my back and I'll scratch yours" idea. On the other hand, we are often convinced that if we make mistakes, God will punish us. These ideas are nothing but the teachings of *religion*. By "religion" I mean the institution of man that focuses on law rather than grace and rules rather than relationship; it has a form of godliness but denies its power. Religion says that if you do right, God will help you, but if you do wrong, He will throw you into hell.

We think that if we go to church God will be happy with us. Going to church can draw us closer to the Lord and make us happy, but it will not by itself make Him happy. That depends on the attitude of our heart. God looks for humble, repentant, and obedient hearts, not showy performance of rituals and busy activity.

The same thing applies to paying our tithe. Some people think they can earn God's favor by giving Him tithes and offerings. God does not need our money. As Creator, He already owns everything. What He looks for are people who give willingly and cheerfully, not only in obedience to His command, but also from a heart overflowing with love and gratitude toward Him. Paul said, *"Let each one do just as he has purposed in his heart, not grudgingly or under compulsion; for God loves a cheerful giver"* (2 Corinthians 9:7).

God does not help us because we go to church, pay our tithe, read our Bible, or do good works. These things are good and appropriate in their place, but they should always rise from the outflow of hearts already made right with God through faith in Christ. If we do any of those things out of a desire to impress God or earn His favor, we are wasting our time.

We cannot earn a miracle. Never will we be good enough to deserve God's favor. There is nothing we can do to merit salvation. Isaiah 64:6 says that in God's eyes *"all our righteous deeds are like a*

48

filthy garment." The stain of our sin has made us unholy and undeserving of anything from God except His condemnation. Only the blood of Jesus can remove that stain. When God blesses us, it is not because we are perfect, but because of His great love and mercy and because we are covered in the righteousness of Christ and use our faith in Him.

God does not do anything for anybody because of their works or how long they have been saved. We don't do God any favors by serving Him. By forgiving our sins and saving us, the Lord has already done infinitely more for us than we would ever have the right to ask. I know people who have been saved for sixty years and couldn't get a miracle. On the other hand, I have seen folks who have been saved for two weeks get so many miracles that it was mind-boggling.

You cannot earn God's blessings. You won't get a miracle just because you have been following the Lord for twenty years. God moves for people who use their faith in Him and who walk in obedience to His Word. Don't let yourself get caught up in the merit system because the merit system is merely religion. You can never be good enough to impress God. Your only hope of tapping into a miracle is to love the Lord with all your heart, sell out to Him completely, and live by faith. This is not religion, but *relationship.*

Change Your Mind-set

"Religious" thinking is a trap that is easy to fall into but difficult to get out of. How do you get rid of religious thinking? Start by establishing the mind-set that you can *never* be good enough to get God to do something for you. None of us can. The merit system has no merit. It carries no weight with God at all. Get it through your head right now that there is nothing you can ever do to earn God's favor.

Fortunately, you don't have to. The moment you trusted in Christ, His blood covered you and cleansed you from sin. When God looks at you now, He does not see your faults, weaknesses, and failures. What He sees is the righteousness of His Son covering your life. In Christ you are adopted into God's family, and all His riches and blessings are yours by right as an heir and family member.

Now that you are in Christ—in a growing relationship with the living, risen Lord—your past with all its mistakes no longer matters.

God has made you a new creature in Christ because He wants to make all things new in your life. Every good father wants the best for his children. Your heavenly Father is the same way, only more so. He wants to see you fulfill your destiny.

Walking by faith as a member of His family, you can depend on your Father to act on your behalf. God will bless you not because you are good or because you deserve it or because you have earned it, but because you are *family*. When my children come to me because they need something, I give it to them not because they deserve it necessarily, but because they are my children. I love them and want to take care of them. We don't get anything from God because of our merit. We get it because He is our Father, and when we go to Him and say, "Daddy, I need Your help," He responds. God acts for us on the basis of our relationship with Him, and for no other reason.

> *"God blesses us because we are family."*

That is why it is so important to know who you are in Christ. Because you are a child of God, all the resources of heaven are available to you. Unless you know who you are, however, they won't do you any good. As long as you are unsure of your relationship with the Lord or how He feels about you, you will not feel confident that whatever belongs to Him belongs to you as well.

In the natural, you may feel like a nobody, but in Christ you are somebody: a child of God and an heir to His kingdom. Before that can make a difference in your life and situation, however, you have to change your mind-set. As long as you believe you are unworthy, you will never believe that God wants to help you. As long as you believe you are a loser who will never amount to anything, you will never believe that God wants to prosper you. You will never make a comeback until you realize that it has nothing to do with how good you are, but everything to do with how good God is.

Do you want to break the cycle of destructive patterns in your life? Change your mind-set. Find out who you are in Christ. Learn your place in God's family, then think and live accordingly.

Remember that the blood of Jesus makes you worthy. Exercise your faith for a breakthrough. Your life will start to turn around once you know that God is not mad at you, that He wants to help you, and that in Christ you are the righteousness of God.

You may be "going through" in your life. That does not necessarily mean that God is punishing you. We bring many storms upon ourselves by our sin and disobedience, but storms are also an unavoidable part of life in a sinful world. You can be living faithfully for the Lord and go through storms too. In fact, when you try to follow Christ, your storms usually increase because you become a target for the enemy.

Just because you are going through some trouble today does not mean that God is getting even with you. On the contrary, He stays with you through it and strengthens you to endure. Jesus said, *"These things I have spoken to you, that in Me you may have peace. In the world you have tribulation, but take courage; I have overcome the world"* (John 16:33). God wants you to know that whatever is going on in your life, His grace is sufficient for you. If you trust Him and follow Him, in due time He will restore everything you have lost.

Stop questioning God's love. Stop questioning His goodness. Stop asking Him "Why?" and start trusting Him. Make up your mind to believe that God truly loves you and is not mad at you. This world is cursed, with troubles everywhere, but Jesus came to redeem you from the curse. He died so that you could live. He became sin so that you could become the righteousness of God. He was condemned so that you could go free. Romans 8:1 says, *"There is therefore now no condemnation for those who are in Christ Jesus."* This means that if you have trusted Christ as Lord of your life, God has issued no condemning sentence against you. Jesus took your sentence in your place, and this was the will of His Father. Why would God do all this for you if He was mad at you?

Stop Feeling Unworthy

God is not mad at you, but are you mad at God? We all experience losses and setbacks in our lives, but the real question is how we react to them. Are you mad at God over your losses? Do you blame

Him for your setbacks? Being angry at God for the storms in your life may be a natural initial response, but it is also a sign of "religious" thinking. When you are caught up in religious thinking, you assume that trouble in your life means that God is mad at you and is punishing you for something.

> *"The only thing that pleases God is our faith."*

Many believers who think this way, when confronted by trouble or setbacks, throw their Bibles down with disgust, saying, "This isn't working!" They stop going to church, stop tithing, and stop praying, because their feeling is, "If all of this is not getting me anywhere, then why bother?" Religious thinking asks, "What's in it for me?" It tries to bargain with God: "Okay, Lord, You see how much I am doing for You. Why don't You return the favor?"

Don't ever make the mistake of getting caught up in this kind of "works righteousness," the kind that says, "If I tithe, God will be happy with me." No, if you tithe, your obedience will open up the windows of heaven and break the curse on your life. "Well, I came to church last Sunday even though I didn't feel like it; now God owes me one. He'll help me make some big sales this week." No, He will help you when you sow your seed, exercise your faith, and put Him first in your life.

Our good deeds do not make God happy with us. The only thing that pleases God is our faith. Hebrews 11:6 says, *"And without faith it is impossible to please Him, for he who comes to God must believe that He is, and that He is a rewarder of those who seek Him."* God-pleasing faith is faith that issues forth in obedience.

Don't worry about trying to find all the right things to do to make God happy with you. You can't. God already loves you with an everlasting love (see Jeremiah 31:3). There is nothing you can do to make God love you more than He already does. Because you are His child by faith in Christ, He delights in you as any father delights in his children.

You cannot make God happy with you because He is already happy with you! You are the delight of His heart. Sure, you have done wrong things that displease Him and grieve His heart; we all have. Sin in your life as a Christian disrupts your fellowship with the Lord, but it does not change your basic relationship with Him. You are still His child. Simply confess your sins and repent, and your fellowship will be restored. Your heavenly Father loves you and will never reject you. *God is not mad at you!*

Job lost everything—his family, his prosperity, and his health—not because God was mad at him, but because God allowed Satan to test him. In the midst of his trouble and pain, Job fell to the ground and began to bless the name of the Lord. He worshiped God despite his setbacks, and God began to turn everything around in his life. In the end, God gave Job twice as much as he had before.

If you are going through trouble today, follow Job's example. Worship God right where you are, in the midst of everything. By doing so you are saying, "Lord, I have faith in You. I am not caught up in 'works righteousness.' I believe in You, and I will trust You to turn my situation around in Your own time and in Your own way. I am Your beloved child. The blood of Jesus covers me and I am now Your righteousness in Him. I am not going to blame You anymore, because I know You love me and that You are not mad at me. Your grace is sufficient for me. When You say 'It is time,' I know my deliverance will come. In due season, I will reap my harvest."

Stop feeling unworthy of God's love and blessings. Like all of us, in yourself you are unworthy, but the blood of Jesus makes you worthy. When the devil accuses you and says, "You are unworthy," the blood of Jesus speaks for you, saying, "You are worthy." It is time to let go of your feelings of unworthiness.

Feeling unworthy will cause you to have a low self-image. A low self-image will keep you from believing that God really loves you and will hold you back from pressing forward into the bright future and destiny He wants for you. Don't get down on yourself. Remember, *God is not mad at you!*

DON'T JUDGE MY FUTURE BY MY PAST

Chapter Six

WATCH YOUR SELF-IMAGE

L ife is tough enough without the uncertainty of knowing where you stand with God. But not knowing who you are in Christ and how God feels about you makes it even harder. We all don't always achieve our goals. We all will, at times, fail, make wrong decisions, and generally mess up. But without knowing who we are as a part of God's family—why, that just makes things a lot tougher. Repeated failures can destroy our self-confidence until we begin to doubt ourselves about everything. Decisions become difficult to make, and then we start second-guessing the decisions we do make. Before long, we are caught in the self-defeating mind-set of believing that we are nothing but a failure. We become convinced that we will never amount to anything.

Proverbs 23:7 says, *"For as he thinks within himself, so he is."* This means that eventually we become what we think of ourselves. If you think you are no good, that's the way you will live. If you believe you are a failure, you will become a failure. If you are convinced that God is mad at you, you will go through life cowed by fear and guilt.

That is why it is so important to believe what the Word of God says about you. Maybe your family has been down on you for years. In the eyes of society you may be a nobody with no prospects and no future. What do they know? Their opinion doesn't matter. What matters is laying hold of who you are in God's eyes. Knowing that God is not mad at you and is on your side can make a tremendous difference in your outlook as you face the realities of everyday life.

Jesus came to lift you out of all the failures, all the hurts, and all the weaknesses of your past. Although you may have failed in the past, that does *not* make *you* a failure. No matter what anybody else says, you are not a nobody. Even if you sometimes feel like you are a low-down, good-for-nothing scoundrel, in God's eyes, you are a VIP. You are important enough to God that He sent His Son to die for your sins so that you could be brought back into right standing with Him. As a born-again, blood-washed believer, you are a child of God, a member of His royal family, and a citizen of His kingdom. The apostle Peter described your status this way:

> *But you are a chosen race, a royal priesthood, a holy nation, a people for God's own possession, that you may proclaim the excellencies of Him who has called you out of darkness into His marvelous light; for you once were not a people, but now you are the people of God; you had not received mercy, but now you have received mercy* (1 Peter 2:9–10).

Of course, Peter's words apply to all Christians. He said, first of all, that as born-again believers, we are a *"chosen race,"* chosen by God to be His *"own possession."* We belong to Him. Second, as a *"royal priesthood,"* we are kings who rule in God's name as well as priests who represent Him before the world. To be a *"holy nation"* means that we are set apart for God's special use. Finally, as the *"people of God,"* we are citizens of His eternal kingdom. In the world we have received no mercy, but now God's mercy is ours through the shed blood of Jesus Christ.

Every day, life bombards us with negative thoughts, words, and experiences. These things can take a heavy toll on our spirits. Other people put us down, and, if we are not careful, we will start to believe them. With all the negativity that constantly surrounds us, sometimes our greatest need is to reprogram our thinking with the Word of God. We need to know, understand, and *believe* what God says about us. His Word can reveal who we really are: *"For the word of God is living and active and sharper than any two-edged sword, and piercing as far as the division of soul and spirit, of both joints and marrow, and able to judge the thoughts and intentions of the heart"* (Hebrews 4:12).

No one knows you the way God does. Not only does He know all your weaknesses, but He alone also knows the seeds of greatness and the potential for success that He has placed in you. That's why His opinion of you is the only one that matters. God's Word is more powerful than all the failures or all the put-downs you have had in life, but you have to get it inside you

> *"We need to know, understand, and believe what God says about us."*

for it to make a difference. You must reprogram your thinking and overwrite the lies and failures of your past with the truth and power of God's Word. Getting the Word of God inside of you, knowing what God says, and speaking it with your mouth in faith will turn your life around.

The Dangers of Low Self-Esteem

Failures are a part of life, but they don't have to define your life. Just because you have failed does not mean you *are* a failure. Depending on your attitude, your failures can become learning experiences that help you on the road to a greater future.

The baggage of your past—all your failures, mistakes, regrets, shame, and guilt—can create serious self-esteem issues that can derail your dreams and halt your forward progress. Low self-esteem can lock you in the past.

Whatever you constantly hear is what you eventually believe. For this reason, you must be very careful what you listen to. If all you hear is negative, you will become negative. If you speak faith, truth, prosperity, success, and victory into your circumstances, those qualities will eventually characterize your life regardless of your current situation. Give great care to what you feed your heart through your eyes, ears, and mind.

The reason some people think so little of themselves is because other people have talked down to them for so long that they now believe what they have been told. Romans 10:17 says, *"So faith comes from hearing, and hearing by the word of Christ."* If you believe that you are a worthless loser, it is only because you have not gotten into God's Word enough to allow it to build you up. Once you know what God has said about you, you will have no problem with self-esteem.

> *"Whatever you constantly hear is what you eventually believe."*

People who are down on themselves usually have problems with marriage, other relationships, and life in general. Rather than examining themselves, they tend to blame everybody else for their problems. The hardest people to love are people who don't like themselves.

All of us struggle with low self-esteem to a certain extent. At one time or another, we all have been abused, treated harshly, talked down to, or oppressed. Whenever we get beaten down in life, we accumulate baggage—hurt, anger, shame, guilt, low self-esteem, jealousy, pride. As time goes on, our baggage becomes a protective wall that we build around ourselves so that nobody can hurt us again. The problem with this is that we isolate ourselves and eventually become loners.

People with low self-esteem tend to be underachievers. Blind to their true potential they get locked into dead-end jobs and move from one bad relationship to another. They date or marry people who are far beneath them and rarely attempt to improve their circumstances. When they do try, they generally fail. Life has beaten them down so much that they have become programmed to believe that they deserve nothing better. They have no idea how beautiful they really are or what great dreams and accomplishments lie hidden inside them, waiting to be released.

What about you? Does any of that sound familiar? Is your career going nowhere? Are you tired of your string of bad relationships but feel helpless to change? Has life beaten you down for so long that you've resigned yourself to things always being this way? Have you lost your ability to dream? Do you assume that the good things of life are reserved for others and not for you? Do you find yourself saying things like, "I could never accomplish what John accomplished," or "I could never own my own home," or "I could never own my own business"?

The film *Seabiscuit*, based on a best-selling book, tells the story of a racehorse that almost everyone wrote off as a non-performer, yet came back to become a champion. Although Seabiscuit was of champion lineage, grandson of the legendary Man-O-War, he failed to rise to expectations. Eventually, he was sold at a rock-bottom price to a businessman named Charles Howard.

With the help of a gifted but eccentric trainer and an oversized jockey with an almost magical way with horses, Seabiscuit made a complete turnaround. Their patient and careful guidance brought out in Seabiscuit all the potential for greatness that the horse had always possessed. At the beginning of the process, Tom Smith, the trainer, said of Seabiscuit, "He has to learn how to be a horse again." Later on, when asked what turned Seabiscuit around, Charles Howard said, "Well, we just gave him a chance. Sometimes all somebody needs is a second chance."

Are you looking for a second chance? Do you need to learn who you are again? Until you understand who you are in Christ, you have no idea what great things are inside you waiting to be born. Life is too important for you to allow a poor sense of self-worth steal your destiny. You need to learn how to dream again. Dig deep into your soul and unearth the dreams that once filled your life with passion and joy. What is your heart's desire? If you could do *anything* with your life, what would it be? Believe it or not, your dreams are not out of reach, no matter what has happened to you in the meantime. God planted those dreams in your heart, and He wants to birth them in your life. He wants to give you a second chance.

Created to Be Unique

Modern society in general suffers from a self-image problem. The human race is in the midst of a severe identity crisis. Our culture exalts the "fact" that we evolved from tadpoles or monkeys and expresses pride at our "enlightenment" over the religious "superstitions" of the past. We have forgotten where we came from. This fact alone is enough to explain why so many of us have so much trouble with self-esteem.

As born-again believers, the time has come for us to get our act together. It is time to learn who we really are in Christ and to reprogram our minds with the Word of God. We must see ourselves through God's eyes and not through the eyes of mankind or society. The Bible explicitly states that we are created in God's image. That alone makes us special. Furthermore, everyone who have given his or her heart and life to Jesus Christ as Savior and Lord has been adopted into God's family. We didn't deserve it, but God looked on us, saw our need, and extended His mercy. He said, "Come on in! I'm adopting you!" Because He has adopted us, we are now sons and daughters of God and Jesus Christ is our elder brother.

We humans all share the common characteristic of being created in God's image. Beyond that, we are all different. God made us that way on purpose. Society, however, preaches the message that there is one "ideal" standard for everyone. To one degree or another, we all have felt the social pressure to dress the same, look the same, talk the same, act the same—even be the same—as everybody else.

God made us unique and different for a reason. You look different from me, and that's good! My interests are different from yours, and that's the way it should be. We are different colors for a reason, and we come from different cultures for a reason. We have different talents, gifts, and abilities for a reason.

If you are a parent, you need to teach your children that they are part of God's family and help them learn to love themselves for who they are in Christ. They need to be secure in the knowledge that God loves them just the way they are and that He made them the way they are for a reason. You cannot teach them this, however, unless you believe it and know it to be true for yourself.

Society gives us many false messages, such as that we should all strive to be a certain size. Guess what? There are a whole lot of beautiful people in the world who aren't a size six! We are who we are. Whether you are a size six or a size sixteen, you ought to be able to look in the mirror and say, "I like you!"

We are not supposed to be the same. Our individual uniqueness is part of God's design. Each of us is different from everyone else in the world. None of us are the same. God used a different mold for each of us.

You are one of a kind. There is no one else in the world exactly like you. For this very reason, no one else in the world can do what God has called you to do. You can touch people no one else can touch. In being yourself, you have absolutely

> *"Our individual uniqueness is part of God's design."*

no competition. That is why you should never be jealous of what someone else has or does. Focus instead on your own unique capabilities and in fulfilling your dreams and destiny in a way no one else can.

However troubled your past may be and however low you may feel about yourself, Jesus came to turn your situation around. He came to assure you that you are a somebody, not a nobody. Sometimes you may feel like a loser, but you are not a loser. The Bible says that you are a joint-heir with Christ, which means that whatever belongs to Jesus belongs to you as well. What's His is yours.

Regardless of your current situation, once you know who you are in Christ, everything can change suddenly. All you have to do is take hold of God's Word and believe that God did not create you to live in failure or to be a slave of your past. He created you for victory. You don't have to stay where you are. What you went through last year you don't have to go through this year.

Rather than continuing to labor under the burden of low self-esteem, make up your mind to live for the Lord. Throw your shoulders back in the knowledge that you are not a worthless failure but a unique individual created in the image of God! He loves you and is not mad at you! Rejoice! You are a joint-heir with Jesus Christ, the King of kings and Lord of lords! He has a wonderful destiny for you, and it can begin today. You don't have to wait six months or a year; you can start right now.

Turning Things Around

Today can be a new day for you. God wants to do something new in your life. Now that you belong to Christ, you are on God's side and He stands ready to help you. No sin you committed, no shameful past memory, no guilty conscience, no failure—no matter how disheartening—is more powerful than the Lord's ability to restore you and turn your situation around. Because you are a child of God, you can overcome the worst that the enemy can dish out: *"You are from God, little children, and have overcome them; because greater is He who is in you than he who is in the world"* (1 John 4:4).

God wants to turn things around for you, but He cannot do it if you have unconfessed or unrenounced sin in your life. As long as you are in a state of disobedience or are not walking by faith, there is little the Lord can do for you. If you seek God, however, and get out of the cycle of sin, you can get into the cycle of blessing. It all depends on *who* and *how* you love.

Everybody wants to be blessed, but few understand how to put themselves in position for it. The key to receiving God's blessings is found in what Jesus identified as the two greatest commandments: *" 'You shall love the Lord your God with all your heart, and with all your soul, and with all your mind.' This is the great and foremost commandment. And a second is like it, 'You shall love your neighbor as yourself' "* (Matthew 22:37–39).

Jesus revealed four things we must do to see God turn things around in our lives: Put God first in everything we do, love God with everything we are, love our neighbor, and finally, love ourselves. The order of priority is very important. If we don't put God first and love

Him supremely, how can we possibly love our neighbor or ourselves? If we do not love our neighbor, whom we can see, how can we love God, whom we cannot see?

If you want to see things change in your life in the area of low self-worth, start by putting God first, loving Him with all your heart, then loving your neighbor as yourself. It does no good to try to love yourself without first learning to love God and then your neighbor.

Do you wonder why God is not blessing you? It may be because you won't break the cycle of sin, guilt, and low self-esteem you are caught up in. Do you go to the Lord for forgiveness when you sin, only to go right back out and do the same thing again? Sin feeds guilt and guilt feeds poor self-worth—it all becomes a vicious cycle. The only way to break that cycle is to make up your mind to get out of sin once and for all, sell out to the Lord, and put Him first in everything. That opens the door for His love to flow, for His blessings to come down, and for His Spirit to work in turning your situation around.

Once you put the Lord first and seek to love Him with all your heart, His love will enable you to love your neighbor. When your life and your love are in alignment with God, you will be able to fully love yourself, and then you will not have anymore problems with low self-esteem. You will know who you are in Christ, you will stop putting yourself down, you will stop feeling bad about yourself, and you will stop falling back into the same old sins. By getting your spiritual priorities right, you will open the door for God to bless your life in every other area. If that's not a turnaround, I don't know what is!

The Power of Our Words

If we are always down on ourselves and speaking negativity into our environment, all we accomplish is the perpetuation of the cycle of circumstances that keep us from getting ahead. There truly is power in our words. According to what we say, we speak either blessings or curses on ourselves.

Jesus said that we should be careful what we say because our words will determine how we come out of our trouble: *"For by your words you shall be justified, and by your words you shall be condemned"* (Matthew 12:37). This principle applies to every area and relationship in life. We must exercise great care in what we say about our spouse, our children, our neighbors, our job, our fellow workers, our church, and our life in general, because what we say, good or bad, has a way of coming to pass.

> *"What we say, good or bad, has a way of coming to pass."*

If we call our spouse stupid or tell one of our children that he will never amount to anything, our words will go into their spirits and cut like a knife. Everything we say either builds up or tears down someone's self-esteem. The futures of many people have been derailed by thoughtless and hateful words. Our words are never neutral; they either justify us or condemn us. We either speak blessings or curses upon ourselves, our loved ones, and our circumstances.

Whether good or bad, words once spoken can never be recalled, and even the negative things we say in private have a way of coming out in time. The writer of Ecclesiastes warned, *"Furthermore, in your bedchamber do not curse a king, and in your sleeping rooms do not curse a rich man, for a bird of the heavens will carry the sound, and the winged creature will make the matter known"* (Ecclesiastes 10:20).

When we murmur, backbite, criticize, or complain, we set ourselves up for tough times because our words will eventually be exposed, resulting in embarrassment, hurt, anger, and animosity. If nothing else, our negative words and attitude will create a negative environment that will affect everyone around us and hinder us from improving our circumstances. We can curse ourselves by our negative words.

The Bible says that we reap what we sow. This is an inescapable principle of life. Ecclesiastes 11:1, the verse that immediately follows the one above, says: *"Cast your bread on the surface of the waters, for you will find it after many days."* The context of this verse is sowing and reaping, and the casting of our bread refers to those things we say in private. Whatever we sow, positive or negative, good or evil, will come back to us after many days. Our words will return to us just as surely as the tide goes out and comes in. When they do, they will be either our glory or our shame, our justification or our condemnation.

If you want to break the cycle of low self-esteem in your life, you may need to change your words. Instead of talking down on yourself and others and constantly harping on why you cannot do something or get ahead, try speaking faith, hope, and confidence into your life and all those around you. Speak *life* into your dead situation.

God told Ezekiel in a vision to prophesy to the valley of dry bones. As Ezekiel obeyed, the bones came together into skeletons. Flesh covered the bones and breath entered the bodies until finally a great army stood before the prophet (see Ezekiel 37:1–10). Through this vision God was telling Ezekiel to speak life into his dead situation.

What is dead in your life that God wants to restore? What "dry bones" has He told you to prophesy life over? Will you obey Him and watch things change, or will you keep on doing what you have been doing? Just as God commanded Ezekiel to prophesy life into his dead situation, so He wants you to prophesy life and good things into all the "dry bones" of your circumstances.

That's what faith is all about. Don't think for a minute that you are exercising faith if you feel you cannot tithe or speak good into your bad situations. Jesus is calling you to believe that your greatest days are still ahead. He wants you to speak that truth into your life starting right now. You have to be able to say it even when things are the worst they have ever been in your life. The Lord has promised that if you change your confession, you will begin the process of seeing things turned around. God has called you to victory, not defeat; to success, not failure; and to life, not death.

Paul says in Romans 8:37 that in all things we *"overwhelmingly conquer"* through Christ, who loves us. People may say you are no good, but God says you are the head and not the tail. You are more than a conqueror through Christ, who loves you. If God says that about you, who are you to argue? Or, as Paul stated it, *"What then shall we say to these things? If God is for us, who is against us? He who did not spare His own Son, but delivered Him up for us all, how will He not also with Him freely give us all things?"* (Romans 8:31–32)

God wants you to get your thinking in alignment with His. If God says you are more than a conqueror, that means you don't have to have a low opinion of yourself anymore. You may have failed in the past, but today you are the righteousness of God. He is not mad at you, He has covered you in the blood of Jesus, and He is on your side. Stop putting yourself down. Instead of always complaining about what you can't do, try declaring along with Paul, *"I can do all things through Him who strengthens me"* (Philippians 4:13)!

You need to change the way you speak because your future is at stake. Whatever you say, good or bad, will come back to you. Rather than saying, "I can't make it," say, "I'm going somewhere. Things may not look good today, I may be in the wilderness, but I'm coming out of this thing. I'm working my way out. If God is for me, who can be against me? This is my year, my hour to get my act together."

God wants you to see yourself through His eyes. Even if you have had more failures than you can count, God doesn't hold your failures against you. He is not mad at you. Now that you are born again, God does not see your filthy rags. He sees the righteousness of Christ covering you. If your attitude is right, you can believe God to do impossible things. With the right attitude, you will be able to claim with confidence, "With God's help, I'm going to turn my life around. My best days are still ahead!"

Chapter Seven

MOVING ON WITH LIFE

Your whole future changed the moment you were born again through faith in the Lord Jesus. In that instant you became a child of God, adopted into God's family, and were clothed in the righteousness of Christ. The blood of Jesus freed you from your sin and from all the disappointment, disillusionment, shame, and failure of your past. His grace and mercy released you to pursue your destiny in Him.

When you were saved, God gave you everything you need for victory and success. This does not mean, however, that just because you are now a Christian, all your struggles and difficulties are over. Rather, the Christian life is a journey of growth toward maturity that involves overcoming many obstacles and fighting many battles. Armed with the Word of God, His constant presence and power through the Holy Spirit, and a new godly nature within you, you must press forward through the combat zone in order to reach your destination.

Of all the struggles you will face on your journey, your hardest fight will be on the battlefield of your own mind. Too often we underestimate the power of our minds and the effects our thoughts can have on our overall health and welfare. In Christ, our ultimate victory is assured.

Victory in daily living, however, is not automatic. It depends on the choices we make and the level of our obedience to the Word and will of God. Our thoughts can make us or break us. That is why it is so important to get our thinking in alignment with the Word of God.

Our spiritual enemy has a way of deceiving us through our minds. All he has to do to control our lives is to provoke us to think wrong thoughts. They manifest themselves in many different ways: negative, critical, and judgmental attitudes; nagging fears and questions; impulsive reactions to the way people treat us; suspicion of others and their motives. Instead of responding in love to the people around us, we end up believing that everyone is out to get us. Satan's goal is to assault us with negative thoughts until we lock ourselves into a self-defeating mind-set of guilt, discouragement, wrong thinking, wrong choices, and inappropriate behavior.

> *"Our thoughts can make us or break us."*

Take a look at yourself. If you seem to be stuck in neutral, unable to get anywhere with your life, you may need to examine your mind-set. Are you a negative person? Do the words you speak tear down yourself and others more often than they build up? Do you *expect* things to go wrong because that's just the way your life goes? Are you quick to find the dark side of every situation? If so, the problem probably stems back to your thought life.

As long as your thinking is contrary to God's Word, you cannot live a productive life. Thinking precedes action. We become what we think of ourselves. Our thoughts determine what we believe, how we see the world, and how we live. How can we live like people of God if we think like the world? On this idea Paul wrote:

> *I urge you therefore, brethren, by the mercies of God, to present your bodies a living and holy sacrifice, acceptable to God, which is your spiritual service of worship. And do not be conformed to this world, but be transformed by the renewing of your mind, that you may prove what the will of God is, that which is good and acceptable and perfect* (Romans 12:1–2).

What we need is a change of mind. We will never act like the chosen race, the royal priesthood, and the holy nation we are in Christ until we start thinking that way.

As a believer, you have the ability to set your mind on the things of God. In fact, Paul said to do exactly that: *"If then you have been raised up with Christ, keep seeking the things above, where Christ is, seated at the right hand of God. Set your mind on the things above, not on the things that are on earth"* (Colossians 3:1–2).

Victory over the crippling mind-set that keeps you mired in the past will come when you decide to cast off negative thinking and take authority over your own mind in Jesus' name. Just being a believer is not enough. Even as a Christian you can still live a totally defeated life unless you make up your mind to stop thinking the wrong things and to stop doing what your worldly mind tells you to do.

God wants you to think right and live right and walk in victory, but He will not do it for you; you have to make the choice. Only you can decide to do what is right. It won't be easy, and at first things may even look as though they are getting worse. Once you have made up your mind to change, however, you will discover that God stands ready to help you. God will never ask you to do something that you cannot do or that He will not equip you to do. He has already made available to you everything you need. In Christ, all things are yours and you can do all things through Him who strengthens you.

As a believer, you have power over your own mind because you have received the mind of Christ (see 1 Corinthians 2:16). Through the Holy Spirit, the fullness of Christ dwells in you (see Ephesians 1:22–23). When you repented of your sins, you were buried with Christ and then raised with Him into a new life and a new freedom. Your past was left behind along with all its regret and failure, as well as its ability to hold your mind captive. You are as free as you want to be, so never judge your future by your past.

God Can Use Anybody

One of the things I love about the Old Testament is the way it shows how God uses weak and ordinary people to accomplish His plan. Just look at the life of David. A great king, a great warrior, a great man of faith who was strong in the Lord, David also had great weaknesses that almost destroyed him on more than one occasion. In addition to wisdom, faith, and love for God, the résumé of David's life also included lust, adultery, and murder. In spite of these things, David was still a man "after God's own heart." Through confession and repentance, David rose above his sins and weaknesses and is forever remembered as Israel's greatest king. If God could use David, He can use anyone.

> "If God could use David, He can use anyone."

Moses could not talk without stuttering, yet God chose him to confront Pharaoh and lead the Israelites from slavery to freedom. Although raised in the royal house of Egypt, Moses fled the country after killing an Egyptian in anger. He spent the next forty years as a wandering shepherd on the backside of the desert. Neither his flaws nor his past mattered when Moses chose to obey and follow God. Moses fell from being a prince of Egypt to a lowly shepherd, but he came back to deliver an entire nation.

Rahab was a harlot, a madam in the red-light district of Jericho. Nevertheless, she cast her lot with the God of Israel by hiding the Israelite spies Joshua had sent. As a result, she and her entire family were spared when the city was destroyed. They became a part of the nation of Israel, and Rahab's name is listed in Matthew's record of the lineage of Jesus.

Whenever you feel down or useless to God because of your past, a look in the Bible at the kind of people God used should be sufficient to lift your spirit. If God could use murderers, prostitutes, tax collectors, fishermen, government officials, political radicals, religious fanatics, physicians—you name it—He can use *anybody*, including *you*. Your past does not matter to God. What matters is your willingness to forget your past, love and follow God with all your heart, and let Him help you build a new and better future.

It's not always easy to change our negative thinking. Old habits are hard to break. The idea that God can and wants to use you in spite of your past may sound too good to be true. Add to the mix all the people around you, especially family members, who try to hold you back by reminding you of your past and all the things you have working against you, and you can easily become overwhelmed with a sense of futility. Sometimes you just have to grit your teeth, get a firm grip on life, and hang in there. Look in the mirror and say, "I'm through reliving the past and I'm through with my negative mind-set. I'm changing my mind to conform to the mind of Christ. I will not allow negative thinking to hold me back anymore."

Never again should you make the mistake of judging your future by your past. In Romans 8:31 Paul asked, *"If God is for us, who is against us?"* Stated another way, we could say this: *If God is for us, nothing in our past can keep us from our future, if we will simply trust and follow Him.*

We have to release our past to the Lord and trust that tomorrow will be better than today. No matter how grim or discouraging your present circumstances may appear, if you love the Lord then you can rest assure that your life is in His hands and He is taking you somewhere. Even though you may not always understand some of the things you go through along the way, remember that God knows what He is doing and has your best interests at heart. His plans for you are for *"welfare and not for calamity to give you a future and a hope"* (Jeremiah 29:11). When you follow the Lord, He accepts you as you are but He will not leave you as you are. Whatever your circumstances, you are on His potter's wheel, and He is shaping you into the person He wants you to be and preparing you for the future He desires for you.

The God of the Bible is a faith God, and when you love Him, He will develop faith inside of you. When He talks to you, rather than focusing on where you have been or even on where you are now, He will talk about where you are going. He will talk to you about starting a business while you are broke. He will talk to you about a husband or a wife even when you have not had a date in five years. He will talk to you about a house of your own while you have little money and few assets.

Isn't it amazing how God will talk to us about our future even when our hopes and our prospects appear to have reached a dead end? We may be so far down that we have to look up to see bottom, and that is when God speaks to us about tomorrow. He is a God who calls things that be not as though they were (see Romans 4:17). While everyone around us harps about our mistakes and tells us all the reasons why we will never amount to anything, God quietly speaks into our spirit about where He is taking us. He speaks to us about our destiny.

Let It Go

One day the Lord spoke to Abram about his future:

Now the LORD said to Abram, "Go forth from your country, and from your relatives and from your father's house, to the land which I will show you; and I will make you a great nation, and I will bless you, and make your name great; and so you shall be a blessing; and I will bless those who bless you, and the one who curses you I will curse. And in you all the families of the earth shall be blessed" (Genesis 12:1–3).

At this time, Abram was already seventy-five years old and his wife, Sarai, who was sixty-five, was also barren. Abram and Sarai had no children and were beyond childbearing age, yet God promised that He would make of Abram *"a great nation"* through whom all the earth would be blessed. Humanly speaking, such a future was impossible for Abram. How could he become the father of a nation if he had no children?

God challenged Abram to look beyond his present circumstances. If Abram was willing to trust God and leave his past behind, then God would take him to a new place of blessing. For Abram this meant leaving his comfortable surroundings and walking by faith to the new land that God revealed to him. Abram believed God and went forth and received his blessing. God gave Abram and Sarai a son, Isaac, from whom descended the nation of Israel. As a sign of Abram's new status, God changed his name to Abraham. Abram means "exalted father," while Abraham means "father of a multitude." When Abram's future changed, he needed a new name to reflect who he had become. God took an apparent dead-end situation and turned it into a glorious, unlimited destiny.

Moving on in your life means letting go of the past. Like Abram, you will need to leave some things behind if you expect to move ahead with the Lord. In order to walk in God's blessings, you will have to leave your comfortable surroundings; you'll have to get out of your "comfort zone." There is comfort in the familiar. When pain or hurt comes into our lives, our natural tendency is to feel sorry for ourselves and revert to our old familiar sinful habits and modes of thinking. That's when the enemy moves in for the kill. Satan plays dirty; he has no qualms about kicking us when we are down.

Whatever you are harboring in your heart that holds you back— self-pity, resentment, a chip on the shoulder, bitterness, anger, shame, bad memories, nostalgia—you have to let it go. God has something new planned for you. You can't travel to the new land while carrying all the baggage of the old. It is only when you let go of the past that you can take hold of the future.

The devil cannot stop God's plan for our lives; if he could, none of us would be saved. God wants to bring us to a new place of blessing, and that requires us to leave the past behind and move forward in faith, trusting the Lord with all our hearts. If you determine to walk by faith, God will bring a river into your desert. You may have made a lot of mistakes and done some pretty stupid things, but with God's help you can move on.

Even if something or someone has died in your life, remember that with God, death is never the end. With God, death is a new beginning. Your new life in Christ began with your death to the old life of sin and your rising to walk in newness of life, as symbolized by your baptism. God has something new for you, and it begins with a right relationship with Him.

Before you can move to a new place of blessing, you must stand strong in the Lord and believe that He is going to turn things around in your life. When you put Him first, He will turn your scars into stars, your pain into promise, and your mess into a message. Simply trust and obey, and God will do something completely new in you.

> *"When you put Him first, He will turn your scars into stars, your pain into promise, and your mess into a message."*

Abram did not know what was waiting for him when he got up to go to a new place, but he did know that whatever it was, God's blessing would be upon it. You may not know exactly what God has in store for you either, but you can be sure that if His blessing is on it, you will have a great life. Getting caught up in keeping track of who said or did what to you will only hold you back. Let go of the past. All that really matters is to forgive, forget, and move on to the place of blessing that God has for us.

Move on to a New Place of Blessing

We never know what lies ahead of us, and that can be scary. Since we tend to fear the unknown, it is easy to cling to the past because, good or bad, the past is familiar and therefore comfortable. God wants to bless us and lead us to a new place, but He cannot if we are always looking back. Blessings are for the future, not the past. Our future may be unknown, but it is not uncertain. God loves us and has our best interests at heart. As we release ourselves into His hands and commit to walk in faith, we can move forward in confidence, knowing that wherever the Lord leads us, we will be safe and secure in His grace.

One of our biggest problems in letting go is that we sometimes take a perverse pleasure in our pain. We love to nurse the hurts of our past. Injured pride keeps us thinking about the people who wronged us, and we rehearse those offenses over and over in our minds. We start avoiding those people. Eventually, we may even lose sleep because we can't let go.

How many blessings from God have *you* missed because you were focusing on the past instead of looking to the future? Don't forfeit any more blessings. Release all your hurts and put them behind you, determined never again to look back. Only then will you be ready and able to move forward into the blessings of God.

The more you rehearse and rehash the past, the more opportunity you create for a vindictive spirit to arise in your heart. If that happens, strife, division, bitterness, and even hatred will follow in short order, providing the very fuel that the enemy needs to destroy you and those around you. When you allow revenge or hatred to control you, you actually give the devil the legal right to destroy you. For this reason, be sure to pay careful heed to the counsel of God's Word. In Ephesians 4:26–27 Paul wrote, *"Be angry, and yet do not sin; do not let the sun go down on your anger, and do not give the devil an opportunity."* Hebrews 12:15 says, *"See to it that no one comes short of the grace of God; that no root of bitterness springing up causes trouble, and by it many be defiled."*

You need the blessings and miracles of God too much to allow bitterness and hatred to stop the flow of His power coming into your life. As long as you indulge the flesh, your life will be out of control. The excess baggage of bitterness, hatred, and unforgiveness will weigh you down so that you never get anywhere. Go to the Lord and learn to walk in love. Drop your baggage by the side of the road. Release from your mind all the people who have hurt you and step forward unencumbered into your future.

Jesus said, *"Love your enemies, do good to those who hate you, bless those who curse you, pray for those who mistreat you"* (Luke 6:27–28). This is the key to our blessings and our future. The Lord expects and even commands us to love and pray for our enemies. This means to pray for the people who have mistreated you, not asking God to change *them*, but to change *you* and your attitude toward them. Healing will come when you lay your bitterness and hatred at the foot of the cross and pray for those who have hurt you.

Our spiritual enemy loves to hold us in the bitterness and pain of our past. His goal is to steal our future and deprive us of God's blessings. We all have hurts in life that we need to get behind us, areas of shame for which we need forgiveness. By the grace of God and through the blood of Jesus we can overcome all things.

The real issue is sin. What are you going to do about it? Will you continue to wallow in the sin and sorrow of the past, or will you obey God and put it behind you in the power of His Spirit? If you are serious about following the Lord and moving into your new place of blessing, then getting rid of bitterness, hatred, and all the baggage of your past is not optional. Unless you turn loose of your grudges and let go of your guilt, you will remain hostage to every hurt, insult, and sin of your past. Life is full of injustices. You must learn to forget them and move on, pressing forward to what lies ahead.

There will come a time in your life when you will have to say, "I am getting up from here. No more moping around for me! My past is over and done; I have too much living to do! I'm on my way to my future, to my new place of blessing!"

In the final analysis, it all comes down to a question of *attitude*.

Chapter Eight

ATTITUDE IS EVERYTHING

If there is one thing that we all share in common as human beings, it is failure. There is not a single one of us who has not failed at something somewhere at some time in our lives. How we respond to failure reveals a lot about our character and our attitude toward life. Although failure can leave us feeling disappointed and discouraged, where we go from there is completely up to us. For many people, failure is a motivator to try harder the next time and to keep on trying until they succeed. Others are devastated by failure and never rise above it.

How does failure affect *you*? Does it motivate you to work harder, or does it cause you to give up in despair? Failure does not define who you are. In the end, whether you overcome failure or it overcomes you will turn on one thing—your *attitude.*

Rather than deal honestly with their failures, many people make excuses and end up never going anywhere. Excuses are for losers. Don't deceive yourself. When you fail in life, it is not because somebody doesn't like you or because you were born on the wrong side of the tracks. It is not because people are against you or because of your skin color. It is not because of where you live or because of who raised you.

You fail when you don't believe the Word of God. You fail when you walk by sight and not by faith. You fail when you allow bad attitudes to get inside you and control you. You fail when you refuse to deal with the baggage in your life—baggage of rejection, pride, low self-esteem, or whatever.

Just because you were abused doesn't give you the right to be mean. Just because you had a rotten family life growing up doesn't give you the right to have a chip on your shoulder. When you came to the Lord with all your baggage, He gave you the strength and the power to deal with all your problems and make all the necessary changes in your life. He expects you to do it.

> *"Your attitude will determine your outcome."*

No matter who you are, life will never live up to all your expectations. Circumstances will disappoint you, and so will people. Friends will let you down and plans won't work out the way you had hoped. Some of your dreams will remain unfulfilled. You may work very hard to reach a certain goal, only to attain it and then look around and say, "Is this all there is?"

One of the biggest challenges you will face in life is keeping a positive attitude in spite of the disappointments that come your way. The real test is how well you can hold on to your faith in the Lord in the midst of trials and testing. Your attitude will make all the difference.

Attitude is everything. Proverbs 23:7 says, *"For as he thinks within himself, so he is."* Whatever you think you are, that is what you are. Your attitude will determine your outcome. If you *think* you won't make it, you *won't* make it; if you *think* your best days are still ahead, your best days *are* still ahead. Whatever you think within yourself is what you will speak into your circumstances, and what you speak is most likely what will take place in your life.

Paul wrote to the Corinthians, *"But thanks be to God, who always leads us in His triumph in Christ, and manifests through us the sweet aroma of the knowledge of Him in every place"* (2 Corinthians 2:14). This means that you can thank God already, no matter what you are going through, because He will cause you to triumph before it's all over.

The Importance of a Good Attitude

Is our attitude really that important? Does it really have that much influence over the course our lives take? Absolutely. People with a poor attitude rarely overcome their problems or failures. For them, life is generally a succession of one defeat after another. People with a positive attitude, on the other hand, usually succeed one way or another, in spite of how circumstances may appear. They have learned the truth from Scripture that says, *"Many are the afflictions of the righteous, but the LORD delivers him out of them all"* (Psalm 34:19).

Whatever your present troubles, let your attitude be, "I will learn from this experience, for I know that in time God will deliver me. My greatest days are still ahead." You may not necessarily see it or feel it, but you need to confess it with your mouth.

As a child did you ever hear the story of "The Little Engine That Could"? Perhaps you have read it to your own children. A little locomotive engine was faced with the task of pulling a heavy load up a long, steep hill. Although he had never tried such a thing before, he did not back away from the job. As the little engine pulled the load and started up the hill, he chugged, "I think I can, I think I can, I think I can..." Even when the climb got harder, he kept telling himself, "I think I can, I think I can, I think I can." Finally, he reached the top. As he started the easy job of going down the other side, he chugged triumphantly, "I thought I could, I thought I could, I thought I could..."

A simple child's story? Of course, but the principle is sound for any age. Few people achieve more than they believe they can achieve. You will never rise higher than your attitude.

Your attitude will determine how well you tap into God's plan for your life. Don't spend another moment wandering around in the desert of defeat! You can't afford it. The Lord has already promised that if you delight yourself in Him, He will give you the desires of your heart (see Psalm 37:4). That means you don't have to be *obsessed* with making money or *consumed* with the pursuit of material things. Wise financial planning and setting legitimate goals are always appropriate, but chasing money and material affluence should never be the driving force of your life. If you will put God first and serve Him with your whole heart, He will provide everything you need. Jesus said, *"Seek first His kingdom and His righteousness; and all these things shall be added to you"* (Matthew 6:33).

Psalm 37:23 says, *"The steps of a man are established by the LORD; and He delights in his way."* As Christians, our lives are under God's control and He establishes our steps; He guides our path. Do you really believe that? If you do, it should affect your attitude about what you are going through right now. You don't have to *like* your current circumstances, but you can rest in the knowledge that God is working things out.

A negative attitude will produce nothing but negative results in your life. That's no way to live. There is no telling what God will do for you if you will simply change your attitude, put Him first in every-thing, and walk by faith. The sky is the limit!

Attitude Determines Altitude

Attitude determines altitude. Your outlook on life influences how high you rise or how far you fall. A negative attitude can squelch your creativity, waste your potential, and derail your dreams. It also can cause you to miss out on the abundant, fruitful, and fulfilled life that God promised and that Jesus came to give you.

One of the saddest stories in the Bible is that of the nation of Israel who were God's people, yet who never entered the promised land. For four hundred years they had been slaves in Egypt until God delivered them through Moses. Even though they were now free, they had trouble letting go of their slavery mind-set. They mur-mured, they complained, they failed to trust God, and they longed to return to the security of Egypt.

The last straw came when they refused to enter Canaan and take the land that God had already promised to them. Seeing the opposi-tion, the Israelites whined, "We're too small and we're too weak. We can't go up against them!" Consequently, God rejected that generation and they wandered in the wilderness for forty years until all those with the rebellious spirit had died. Their "grasshopper" mentality kept them out of their promised land; their bad attitude derailed their destiny.

"Learn to speak faith even when you don't feel faith."

Like the children of Israel, do you suffer from a "grasshopper" mentality? Has life beaten you down until your obstacles seem so big and your strength so small that you feel it is useless even to try to get ahead anymore? Do you wonder why nothing ever changes, even though you are believing God to turn things around? You love the Lord, so why do you never get healed? Why are you always broke, unemployed, or stuck in dead-end jobs? How do you keep getting into one bad relationship after another? Why can't you break the cycle? The answer may very well lie with your attitude.

If nothing changes no matter how hard you try, it's time to stop and examine yourself. Don't make excuses or try to blame somebody else for why you are where you are. The person responsible is the one you see in the mirror every morning. Don't worry, God still loves you even when you complain, but He cannot do much for you. As long as you remain negative, you will stay in the wilderness. Learn to speak faith even when you don't feel faith. It is when things look darkest that you should affirm, "My best days are still ahead."

Your attitude always takes you somewhere, either lower than where you were or higher than where you were. God wants you to be blessed, to grow in Him, and to rise to a higher level spiritually, emotionally, physically, financially, and in every other possible way. If you will cling to the Word of God, make some positive changes in your attitude and behavior, and walk by faith, then today can be the beginning of the best years of your life.

It is never your circumstances that defeat you, but your attitude and your disobedience to the Lord. All it takes for you to lose is to murmur, complain, backbite, or steal the tithe. You are headed for defeat whenever you refuse to forgive someone you need to forgive or release a bad situation you need to release.

Airplanes are equipped with an attitude indicator that tells the pilot the angle of the aircraft's nose. As long as the nose is up, the plane is climbing. A down angle indicates that the plane is descending. If the nose stays down too long, the aircraft will crash.

Many of us have had our noses down so long that we are in imminent danger of crashing on the rocks. That is what can happen whenever we take our eyes off the Lord. When Peter stepped out of the boat to walk on the water to Jesus, he didn't begin to sink until he dropped his gaze from his Master's face to the waves lapping at his feet. Suddenly, his situation looked impossible and he began to flounder. When he looked once more to Jesus, he was lifted up again.

If you have been looking down for a long time, get your attitude indicator in the up angle. Get your eyes back on the Master. Get back into a right relationship by putting Him first in everything every day. The Lord wants you to grow to the point where you can look at any kind of trouble and still keep a positive attitude. He wants you to believe that He is so big that nothing can stop you from being blessed. His desire is that you cast all your cares on Him because He cares for you and will work everything out.

A positive attitude means that even if things look bad now, you will stop believing the worst and start believing that God is turning your situation around. It means believing that everything you are going through is training for where the Lord is taking you. After all, it is not what happens *to* you that determines your future, but what happens *inside* you.

We all go through the wilderness from time to time. It may not be fun, but it is our training ground. In the wilderness is where we learn to tithe, because we can't get out until we do. In the wilderness is where we learn to stop being negative, because we can't get out until we start confessing our faith in the Lord. In the wilderness is where we learn to let go all the issues we have with people who have hurt us, because we can't carry that baggage into the promised land. In the wilderness is where we learn to deal with ourselves.

Attitude Is Everything

Tipping the Balance

Life is unpredictable and often unfair. Many times we are subjected to forces or events beyond our control. Even though we may have little control over what happens to us, we have complete control over how we *respond* to what happens to us. Our attitude requires daily adjustment. Every morning we should set our attitude indicator so we don't crash during the day. This is a deliberate decision on our part to maintain a positive, faith-filled outlook no matter what happens.

A positive attitude is a lifestyle that you must carefully and deliberately nurture. It takes more than just words. You can say, "My best days are still ahead," five hundred times a day, but nothing will change until you make up your mind to change. The first step is a daily decision to put God first—to get into His Word and spend time with Him in prayer on a daily basis.

Aligning your attitude with the Lord first thing in the morning will help you walk in faith, positive thinking, and victory all day long. A positive attitude will make it much easier for you to let go of the past, forgive people who have hurt you, and be a witness for Christ on your job and wherever else you go. Getting your spiritual priorities in order will also help you make the commitment to change in other areas of your life: to lose weight, stop smoking, stop drinking, get off of drugs, go back to school, find a new job, or whatever.

Maintaining a positive attitude makes a world of difference in the area of human relationships. Positive people relate to others better than negative people do, and they are more fun and inspiring to be around. Teddy Roosevelt said, "The formula for success is knowing how to get along with other people." In other words, our success is determined by the way we treat others. Our Lord said, *"Give, and it will be given to you; good measure, pressed down, shaken together, running over, they will pour into your lap. For whatever measure you deal out to others, it will be dealt to you in return"* (Luke 6:38).

Whatever we give to others is what God gives back to us. Galatians 6:7 says, *"Do not be deceived, God is not mocked; for whatever a man sows, this he will also reap."* Seed always reproduces after its own kind. Harsh, unforgiving, negative, or unloving people will reap the same. People who are kind and loving will find kindness and love returned to them.

The point of life is giving. Negativity takes and never gives; it takes our energy, our enthusiasm, our confidence, our trust, our happiness, our hope, and even our health. A positive spirit, on the other hand, not only strengthens and nurtures all of these things in us, but it also helps spread them to others. We will never be happier than when we are living a life of giving rather than a life of taking.

> *"The point of life is giving."*

A positive attitude will help you keep pressing on when someone else might quit. It will help you hang onto your faith, even during difficult times. After all, it is not your difficulties that defeat you, but your negative attitude. Your attitude will either leave you in the wilderness or lead you out; the choice is yours.

God does not want us to sit around regretting our past or worrying about our future. He wants us to cast our cares on Him, put Him first, and live a life of prayer and praise so that He can fight our battles for us. What the devil meant for our destruction, God will turn around for our good. He may not always show up when we want Him to, but He always shows up on time. Even in the midst of trials, we can be confident that if we are serving the Lord faithfully, at some point everything will turn around. If we sow in the winter, we will harvest in the spring.

No matter what you are going through, you are closer to victory than you think. Paul said, *"Let us not lose heart in doing good, for in due time we shall reap if we do not grow weary"* (Galatians 6:9). Don't give up now. Don't let a negative attitude win the day. Your victory is just around the corner. Victory is so close, in fact, that your attitude could tip the balance one way or the other. A negative attitude will keep you wandering in the desert, while a positive attitude will lead you into the promised land.

Attitude Adjustment

It's said that tough times never last, but tough people do. When you have the right attitude about life, you will realize that all the "stuff" you go through is simply God's way of building you up and preparing you to go to another level. As I've said before, the Lord accepts you where you are, but He will not *leave* you where you are.

As we follow the Lord, He sometimes allows things to dry up in our lives until we feel like we are stranded in the desert. Sometimes He removes all visible means of support so that we will learn to trust in Him alone. Always He is training and conditioning us, preparing us to rise to the next level.

Did your job dry up? Do your immediate prospects appear slim? Don't despair! God is getting ready to take you to a new place. If the Lord is first in your life, you need not worry about the state of the economy or about how to take care of your family. God has promised to provide all your needs. Tests and trials come, but that is where we discover how big God really is. It is when we reach the end of our rope and all our resources are exhausted that we come to know God's limitless provision.

Hard times bring out either the best or the worst in us. Nothing reveals our true character like a little pressure. In a way, we are like tea bags—we have to pass through some hot water before our full flavor comes out. God allows us to be tested and tried so we can grow strong in our faith and in our ability to endure. He wants us to come to the place where we can face any situation with the confident assurance that we will prevail in His strength.

No giant is too great to handle when we look at it through God's eyes. Goliath taunted Israel and mocked God, but no one would go up against him because the giant warrior looked too big to defeat. Young David saw things differently. Sizing up the strutting Philistine, David's attitude was, "Man, he's too big to miss! Get me my sling-shot!" It was this same David who said, *"Even though I walk through the valley of the shadow of death, I fear no evil; for Thou art with me"* (Psalm 23:4). It's all about attitude. You may be going through hell and high water, but your attitude should be, "The Lord is with me, and He will lead me safely through!"

We all need regular attitude adjustments because our attitude determines whether we succeed or fail. Why let the past wreck your present or your future? There is nothing you can do about the past except let it go. As long as you look at your circumstances through the eyes of your flesh, all you will see is failure and inadequacy. When you look through the eyes of faith, however, you will be able to exclaim, "My God will always cause me to triumph in Christ!"

Your attitude will either make you or break you. Failure is a part of life but it does not have to define your life. You may have no control over *what* happens, but you do have control over how you respond. In the movie *Seabiscuit*, newspaper reporters ask Charles Howard how he feels after his horse has just lost a race by a nose. Howard replies, "Everybody loses a couple, and you can either pack up and go home, or you keep fighting!" How will *you* deal with failure? Will you view it as a catalyst to get back up and keep fighting or as an excuse to stay down on the canvas?

Thomas Edison failed thousands of times before he succeeded in inventing the lightbulb. The secret to success is never letting failure have the last word. After all, failure is nothing more than a *temporary* setback. There is really very little difference between success and failure. In the Olympic Games, for example, the difference between first and last place—success or failure—may be only one-tenth of a second. Many people give up without knowing they are only a hairsbreadth away from success.

In the summer of 2003, when American bicyclist Lance Armstrong was on his way to his fifth straight victory in the grueling Tour de France bicycle race, he crashed during one of the later stages of the race after his handlebar clipped a spectator's bag. After he went down, he could have said, "Well, that's it." Instead, he got back up, got back on his bike, and told himself, "Lance, if you're going to win this thing, it has to be today." He went on to win that stage and the race itself.

That's the attitude for success. Lance Armstrong did not let a temporary setback keep him down. It should be the same with you. With the right attitude, you will get back up when you are knocked down. You will learn to regard failure as your teacher. Maintaining the right attitude will help you learn how to grow in the midst of your failures. You will learn to look beyond your circumstances to God's provision.

Attitude Is Everything

The facts may say that you are broke, busted, and disgusted, but with the right attitude you will know that when you put God first, He will open up the windows of heaven over your life, and you will not be broke forever. The money may not be there right now, but by sowing in the winter, you will reap in the spring. You may be going through testing now, but keep trusting the Lord anyway. It may be hard to understand why He hasn't answered your prayers yet, but hang in there. Keep your attitude indicator up and exercise your faith. In due season you will reap an abundant harvest.

DON'T JUDGE MY FUTURE BY MY PAST

Chapter Nine

GET READY TO BOUNCE BACK

When you first became a newborn Christian, did you believe that because you now belonged to Christ, all your troubles were over and nothing but smooth sailing lay ahead? You weren't the only one. Even some churches teach this. Unfortunately, this is not the case. Any believer who has spent any time at all in the "trenches" understands that being born again is no shield against trouble. On the contrary, being a Christian in a non-Christian world brings its own unique challenges.

To one degree or another, we who follow Christ should expect the world to treat us the way it treated Him. Jesus told His disciples, *"If the world hates you, you know that it has hated Me before it hated you. If you were of the world, the world would love its own; but because you are not of the world, but I chose you out of the world, therefore the world hates you"* (John 15:18–19). In his first letter, the apostle John explicitly stated, *"Do not marvel, brethren, if the world hates you"* (1 John 3:13).

This present world, for the time being, is under the sway of a spiritual enemy who not only hates God and everything He stands for but also hates everyone who loves and follows God. This is why we can love the Lord with all our hearts and still have setbacks in our lives. We don't have to be in sin to see difficulties come our way. The fact that we know Christ and seek to serve Him faithfully is enough to guarantee that we will face trials.

Godly people in both the Old and New Testaments of the Bible suffered great tribulations for no other reason than that they were living for God. Paul spoke from personal experience when he wrote to Timothy, *"Indeed, all who desire to live godly in Christ Jesus will be persecuted"* (2 Timothy 3:12). Our enemy will come against us simply because of our faith in the Lord.

It is discouraging enough to face trouble because of a mistake you made, but what about the times when a storm hits you for no apparent reason? You have been praying, giving your tithe, and trying to live right and honor the Lord. Just when things are looking bright, the roof caves in. You get fired from your job or evicted from your house. Your spouse walks out on you or one of your children becomes addicted to drugs. You go through a serious health crisis that depletes your financial resources. Suddenly, your whole world has collapsed around you. In desperation you cry out, "Why, God? Why did You let this happen?"

So often it seems as though the devil attacks us the hardest when we are on the brink of a major breakthrough in our lives. Setbacks usually occur just outside the promised land. As the saying goes, it is always darkest right before dawn. Keep in mind that Satan is out to steal your future. So if he is attacking you, don't be discouraged. It just means that God is getting ready to bring a change in your life to lead you to a higher level.

Don't sweat over your trials and tribulations; everybody has them. Instead, trust in the Lord with all your heart, for in Him lies your victory. Jesus said, *"These things I have spoken to you, that in Me you may have peace. In the world you have tribulation, but take courage; I have overcome the world"* (John 16:33).

In Christ you can overcome because He is stronger than any earthly power or principality. John wrote, *"You are from God, little children, and have overcome them; because greater is He who is in you than he who is in the world"* (1 John 4:4). The word *them* in this verse refers to the spirit of antichrist—all who deny Jesus, whether spiritual beings or human beings. Because Jesus overcame the world, you can too.

From Setback to Comeback

Despite the reality of persecution and tribulation that we may face simply because we are believers, the truth is that we bring most of our trials and difficulties on ourselves. Most of the trouble we go through is a result of our own sin, rebellion, and disobedience. Just as we cannot defy the law of gravity by jumping out a second-story window without paying the consequences, neither can we defy God's moral and spiritual laws and get away with it.

Regardless of the reason they come, setbacks are an inescapable reality of life. At one time or another life throws all of us a sucker punch that leaves us reeling and staggering backwards. You may be tripping merrily along with everything going well when suddenly— *pow!*—and you're flat on your back looking up from the canvas into the leering face of adversity.

One of the amazing things about God is that He loves us so much that He wants to help us get back everything we've lost. Whether the devil stole it from us or whether we foolishly threw it away because of our sin and disobedience, God wants to restore what we once had: *"Then I will make up to you for the years that the swarming locust has eaten, the creeping locust, the stripping locust and the gnawing locust, My great army which I sent among you"* (Joel 2:25).

God has a way of taking our setbacks and turning them into comebacks. Regardless of what you have been through, God can take your past and use it for His glory. Even when you have failed in life or missed the mark, even if your goals and dreams seem farther away than ever before, God can bring you back. He has promised that if you put Him first—trust Him and acknowledge Him in all your ways—He will direct your paths (see Proverbs 3:5–6).

We walk by faith, not by sight (see 2 Corinthians 5:7). In other words, setbacks do not mean that our faith is not working. The presence of failure does not mean that God is idle or absent. God is always working for His purpose and our good. For our part, we must learn to distinguish the difference between *fact* (or evidence) and *truth*.

The *facts* may say that you can't pay your bills, but the truth is that *"God shall supply all your needs according to His riches in glory in Christ Jesus"* (Philippians 4:19). Evidence may indicate that the doctors cannot help you, but the truth is that *"He Himself took our infirmities, and carried away our diseases"* (Matthew 8:17). It may appear that all is lost, but the truth is that God is in the process of turning everything around.

> *"Learn the difference between fact and truth."*

When God is working in our lives, He often allows us to go through the fire in order to get our attention. He even uses our failures to help us learn to trust Him. The fire purifies us by burning away things in us that should not be there: unholy thoughts and habits that keep us from following the Lord with our whole heart. Failure teaches us that we are insufficient on our own and that we need God's guiding hand and wisdom to succeed in life.

Everything you experience in life helps prepare you for your future. As a follower of the Lord, you are on His potter's wheel, and He is shaping you into the vessel He wants you to be—a vessel suitable to contain His glory (see 2 Corinthians 4:6–7). Sometimes the shaping process hurts, but the end result is well worth the pain. You will never fully understand why you are on the potter's wheel until you can affirm with David, *"It is good for me that I was afflicted, that I may learn Thy statutes"* (Psalm 119:71). The Lord is working to turn your setbacks into comebacks. Part of the process is for you to learn to say with conviction, "It was good for me to go through the fire."

These Made a Comeback

If you are like me, there have been times when you felt you had sinned so much or failed so badly that you could never recover. Once life beats up on you for a while, it becomes easy just to give up. The only true failures are the people who quit trying.

Get Ready to Bounce Back

In *Seabiscuit*, Tom Smith, the gifted horse trainer, rescues an apparently worthless horse from being shot by its owner. Later, when Charles Howard asks him why he saved the animal, Smith replies, "You don't throw a whole life away just because it's banged up a little." No matter how "banged up" you are by sin or adversity, you can still turn around. As the story of *Seabiscuit* illustrates, *you are never too far behind to come back.*

Are you bothered by the sin in your life? Take it seriously. Confess it to God, but don't feel like you are alone. Sin is the universal condition of man, as Paul made clear when he wrote, *"For all have sinned and fall short of the glory of God"* (Romans 3:23). If that was the end of the story, we would all be in trouble. God, however, did not let things rest there. Paul told us that believers have the *"righteousness of God through faith in Jesus Christ...being justified as a gift by His grace through the redemption which is in Christ Jesus"* (Romans 3:22, 24).

We all have sinned, but by God's grace and through faith in Christ we can make a comeback. This promise is for *everyone* who believes, not just some. No matter who you are, when you trust in the Lord, your ultimate victory is assured: *"Thanks be to God, who gives us the victory through our Lord Jesus Christ"* (1 Corinthians 15:57).

The Bible is full of people who fell short but had great comeback stories. Don't forget about Moses who, although a murderer, fugitive, and obscure shepherd for forty years, came back to deliver his fellow Israelites from slavery in Egypt and lead them to the borders of the promised land. Moses gave to the people the Law, which he received from the hand of the Lord, and even became known as the friend of God. If Moses made a comeback, you can too.

David came back from lust, adultery, and murder to many more years of effective leadership as Israel's king. Through confession and repentance of his sin, David was restored to the fellowship with God he had previously enjoyed, and he continued to be a man after God's own heart. If David made a comeback, you can too.

Joseph's story is a little different. Through no sin or fault of his own, Joseph was sold into slavery by his brothers and endured years of false imprisonment. At all times, Joseph maintained his integrity and his faith in God. Even while he was subjected to such injustice, God was preparing him for a great future. Eventually, God caused Joseph to rise to prominence as the most powerful official in Egypt, second only to Pharaoh himself.

"You are never too far behind to come back."

From this position, Joseph was instrumental in preserving the people of Egypt and the surrounding region, including his own family, through a time of great famine. When Joseph had the opportunity to take revenge on his brothers, he chose forgiveness and mercy instead, understanding that all that had happened to him was God's way of preparing him for his destiny. If Joseph made a comeback, you can too.

The Book of Job relates what is certainly one of the greatest comeback stories in all of Scripture. Job lost everything. In one day he lost his wealth, his health, and his family. All he had left was his faith in God, and that proved to be enough. God had allowed Satan to test Job's faith and integrity to the very limit, and Job passed the test. What the devil meant for Job's destruction, God turned to Job's good.

In the end, God gave Job double for his trouble. He restored to Job twice what he had lost: twice the wealth and twice as many children. God also fully restored Job's health. Through it all, Job steadfastly maintained his faith, even saying at one point, *"Though He slay me, I will hope in Him"* (Job 13:15). This was Job's way of saying, "I've lost a lot. I didn't know if I could make it, but with God's help I will bounce back." If Job made a comeback, you can too.

When you are in the wilderness trying to understand why God is letting you go through trials and difficulties, remember that He is preparing you for something greater. There are some things that God has for you that you will not be ready for until you have passed through the fire. When it's all said and done, you will be able to help other people in a way that would have been impossible before. If you allow it, tribulation will teach you patience, humility, and trust—all of which will make you more usable to God in His plan to reach the whole world with the good news of Jesus Christ.

Stop believing the worst about your situation and start trusting God for a comeback. Give God complete charge of your life, and He will give you the peace of knowing that He will work everything out in His time. When you are walking by faith, you can't judge your circumstances by what you see. You simply have to trust that the Lord is working behind the scenes even when you can't see Him.

Weathering the Storm

Isn't it interesting how God often uses trouble as our ticket to promotion? Tribulation becomes the gateway through which He takes us where He wants us to go. Storms come into every life and, even though we may not like them because of the upheaval they bring, they also bring nourishing, life-giving rain. It is the storm that brings the power of the Holy Spirit into our lives and strengthens us so that we can bounce back. Only by passing through the storm can we move on to our destiny.

Jesus and His disciples were in a boat crossing the Sea of Galilee when suddenly a storm arose, a fierce gale of the sort that is quite common on that lake. So strong were the winds that the boat was in danger of being swamped by the waves. With Jesus sleeping peacefully in the stern, the disciples faced a decision, the same one we face in the middle of a storm: Do we press on or do we turn back? Fearing for their lives, the disciples woke Jesus, who first rebuked the wind and calmed the sea, then rebuked His disciples for their lack of faith (see Mark 4:36–41).

Upon reaching the other side of the lake, they encountered a demon-possessed man who lived among the tombs. The disciples witnessed a miracle as Jesus cast out a legion of demons from the man. Crossing the lake once again, Jesus and His disciples were approached by Jairus, the leader of the local synagogue, who pleaded with Jesus to heal his daughter, who was dying. On the way to Jairus' house, Jesus met a woman who had been sick for twelve years with a hemorrhage. As soon as the woman touched the hem of Jesus' garment, she was healed. In the meantime, Jairus' daughter died, but Jesus raised her to life again.

All of these were great miracles that the disciples might never have experienced had they not first passed through the storm. God can use our storms for our good. No matter what you are going through, keep pressing toward the prize that God has for you. Today you may be in a storm, but there will be bright sunshine tomorrow. God will turn everything around, and you will bounce back.

Remember that what matters is not what happens to you, but how you respond. It doesn't matter how far you have fallen as long as you are determined with God's help to bounce back. When a basketball player misses a shot, he tries to get the rebound so he can make another shot. Life is the same way. Sometimes you miss your goals, but you have to keep trying for the rebound until you make it. This means never quitting, never giving up, and never losing confidence that ultimately you will prevail.

Despite what the devil would have you believe, life is not over just because you have had some setbacks and have not achieved your goals. Although God's plan is for you to bounce back, it will never happen until you make up your mind to do it. God will not force His way on you; He will let you continue in the same self-defeating attitude and lifestyle if you so choose.

As soon as you decide that you have had enough of loss and defeat and turn your heart and mind to the Lord, He will begin then and there to turn things around. It may not happen overnight, but as you trust and follow Him, it *will* happen. God will replace all that the swarming, creeping, stripping, and gnawing locusts have eaten. He will bring back the joy you once knew. He will turn your finances around. The Lord will restore the years that you have lost, not so much in chronological age as in making up for lost time.

It all boils down to faith—trusting the Lord. Some people believe that the faith message is about getting everything they want. These are the "name it and claim it" folks. The *real* faith message, however, is that no matter what happens, you keep serving God anyway. You continue to trust God even when you do not get what you are believing for. Setbacks are only temporary. Every storm, no matter how dark, eventually passes away, and calm seas lie beyond.

Get Ready to Bounce Back

Anybody can quit once they have missed the mark, but God is looking for people who will exercise their faith and be determined to bounce back. He seeks those who will repent of their sins, set their minds to overcome their past, and believe Him for a fresh start.

Once you make up your mind to bounce back, nothing can stop you. After all, if God is for you, who can be against you? Even the devil himself is not strong enough to hold you down because He who is in you is greater than he who is in the world.

With God's help you can rise above your problems and your failures, your prejudice and your low self-esteem. With God's help you can get off drugs and break every addiction in your life. With God's help you can get out of debt and own your own property or even your own business.

Get ready to bounce back. It's time to turn your setbacks into comebacks and move into a new day. It's time to dream again. If you repent and turn to God today, He will turn everything around tomorrow. It's time to start building for a great future.

DON'T JUDGE MY FUTURE BY MY PAST

Chapter Ten

IT'S TIME TO BUILD
FOR YOUR FUTURE

God wants to do a new thing in your life. In order to embrace the new, however, you must be willing to let go of the old. Jesus said, *"No one puts new wine into old wineskins; otherwise the wine will burst the skins, and the wine is lost, and the skins as well; but one puts new wine into fresh wineskins"* (Mark 2:22). You must leave your past behind you and move on. As long as you sit dejectedly amidst the debris of your crushing failures, shattered hopes, and broken dreams, you will never get anywhere. It is only when you make up your mind to step out of the rubble and no longer judge your future by your past that you will be ready to build toward God's new dream for you.

It is one thing to feel sorry about the sins, mistakes, and failures of your past. It is quite another to continue to feel sorry for yourself in the aftermath, especially when God has said that He forgives you and is not mad at you. If God does not hold your past against you, why should you?

God promised that if we will confess our sins, He will forgive us. Take Him at His word. The past is dead; it's time to hold a funeral and bury it once and for all. Only then can you move on to the promises of God. Drop your self-pity, pick yourself up, and start acting like a child of the King. God wants to do a new thing in your life. The question is, are *you* ready?

Usually the past must die before the future can come to life. For the children of Israel, Moses represented the old way of doing things. It was necessary for him to die before they could begin their new life in the promised land:

> *Now it came about after the death of Moses the servant of the LORD that the LORD spoke to Joshua the son of Nun, Moses' servant, saying, "Moses My servant is dead; now therefore arise, cross this Jordan, you and all this people, to the land which I am giving to them, to the sons of Israel"* (Joshua 1:1–2).

A new land calls for new ideas and new ways:

> *Do not call to mind the former things, or ponder things of the past. Behold, I will do something new, now it will spring forth; will you not be aware of it? I will even make a roadway in the wilderness, rivers in the desert* (Isaiah 43:18–19).

Isn't it interesting how we can have our lives all planned out only to have God change the plan? As the children of Israel approached their promised land, the land of Canaan, they were full of hope and faith. Behind them lay forty years of wilderness wandering. Now a new generation had arisen who was eager to go in and possess the land. All of a sudden, Moses, their beloved and trusted leader, died. The Israelites were on the verge of victory when they suffered a tremendous setback. At least, that is probably the way they looked at it. After all, Moses had led them out of Egypt, had given them the Law from God, and had represented them before God for forty years. What would they do without him?

Very simply, they would continue on under a new leader, Joshua. What the Israelites saw as a setback God saw as a natural

100

and necessary transition in order for His people to move to the next level. God had something totally new planned for them, but before they could claim it, they had to bury their past.

Bury the Dead Things

Isn't it much easier sometimes to simply stay where you are rather than move forward? Sometimes the future is scary. Most of us tend to find comfort in the familiar, even when it is not pleasant. We would rather stay in the comfortable past than venture into the frightening future with all its unknowns. Nevertheless, progress lies ahead of us, not behind us. We must bury the past; otherwise, it will keep drawing us back.

> *"The past is dead; it's time to hold a funeral and bury it once and for all."*

After the Israelites crossed the Red Sea on dry land, God closed the waters behind them. This was not only to protect them from the Egyptian army, but also to shut off any avenue for them to return to their former life. Their past was dead. Their future lay before them. God knew that the hardship and uncertainty the people would face in the days ahead would cause many of them to long for the old days.

There are times in our lives when God closes the door on some past things so that we cannot go back even if we want to. He may close one door in order to open another, but His way always leads forward. Our proper response is to follow in faith.

After Moses died, the Israelites mourned him for thirty days. God then told Joshua that the time of mourning was past. It was time for them to move into their promised destiny. They were to dry their tears, cross the Jordan, and take possession of the land of Canaan for themselves.

Mourning is a normal and natural human response to loss. We all grieve when a loved one dies or when we go through a divorce or other broken relationship. What is *not* normal is to get stuck in our grief and never get beyond it. If the Israelites had never stopped mourning for Moses, they would never have gotten out of the wilderness.

Have you ever felt a pain of loss so intense that you thought you would never recover? Have you ever been so paralyzed by overwhelming grief that you could not function normally? Does sorrow over your past seem to hold you in a death grip? You will never be able to rise to the new things that God has for you until you can let go of your mourning, dry your tears, and bury your dead past.

Often, burying our past is easier said than done. Sometimes it is very hard to leave the past behind. Don't give up. The Lord stands ready to help you. If you are having trouble letting go, turn your problem over to God. He will help you make peace with your past by plunging it under the blood of Jesus. Once you have made peace with your past, you can bury it and move on.

One time a man expressed a desire to follow Jesus, but wanted to *wait* until after his father died. Jesus said to him, *"Follow Me; and allow the dead to bury their own dead"* (Matthew 8:22). He was not telling the man to ignore his responsibilities to his parents. Rather, Jesus was warning him that his desire to hold on to his old life threatened to prevent him from following the new life to which he had been called.

The Lord has called you to a new life, to a new and living future, but you risk missing it if you refuse to bury the dead things of your past. As long as you continue to sit by the graveside, you cannot move to the new place God has for you. What are you grieving over today? The years you have wasted to drugs or alcohol? The shame of sexual sin? Years of poor lifestyle choices that have damaged your health? The death of a spouse or a child? A broken relationship? Painful memories? Whoever or whatever you are mourning, it is time to let go. Bury your grief under the grace of God and the blood of Jesus and move on into your new destiny in the Lord.

You may have to make up your mind to stop dating certain people or hanging around certain places. The longer you linger near dead situations, the more dead you will act. Old memories, good or bad, are like an old pair of shoes that you would like to throw away, but cannot. You don't really want them anymore, but they are so comfortable that you cannot bring yourself to get rid of them. It's time to bury the dead things of your past. As comfortable as your past may seem, in order to build a new life, you have to leave the safety of your comfort zone.

Created to Be Builders

Centuries ago, God instructed Noah to build an ark to protect himself and his family from the great flood that was coming to destroy all life on the earth. Noah took God at His word and obeyed. By building the ark, Noah was building for the future—not only for himself, but also for the entire human race. Noah's obedience was critical because time was running out. What would have happened if Noah had procrastinated or spent too much time grieving over the world that was about to be lost? His future lay beyond the flood, but to get there he had to build the ark.

Like Noah, your future lies beyond the storms of the present, and you cannot get there by shoring up the fallen structures of the past. What kind of "ark" are *you* constructing for yourself and your family? Are you building your life properly? Are you using the right materials? Is your "ark" based on the values and philosophies of the world or on the unchanging Word and promises of God? How you answer is very important. This is no time to play around; the hour is late.

It is time to get serious with God, to stop riding the fence and get your life turned around. There is a storm just over the horizon and God is warning you to be prepared. He has a bright future planned for you, but it won't happen without your willing participation.

If you are going to walk in your destiny, you need to be building toward the future all the time. God is a builder and He created us to be builders. In the beginning, God gave Adam and Eve dominion over the earthly realm and charged them to *"be fruitful and multiply, and fill the earth, and subdue it"* (Genesis 1:28). In other words, they were to take the world they were given and build from it an even greater realm that would reflect their God-given gifts and creativity.

God created us in His own image, and we can never truly be happy unless we are following His will. We are builders by design, and we find fulfillment only when we are building. Being stuck in the past is stagnation, and stagnation is only one level above death.

It is no accident that Jesus was raised as a carpenter. That was God's way of showing us that He is in the building business. As children of God, His business is our business. We are builders, but as long as we live in guilt and condemnation, we will never build anything. God designed each of us to be extraordinary in our own way. Although we are all different, we each possess the capacity in Christ to build a future that overcomes every obstacle in our path.

> *"You need to be building toward the future all the time."*

Build on the Right Foundation

The most important part in the construction of any building is the foundation. Nothing can compensate for a flawed foundation, not even the finest architectural plans or the highest quality building materials. A poor foundation will undermine the entire structure.

Life is the same way. Unless we build on a proper foundation, we are doomed to failure. Jesus illustrated the importance of a sound foundation in the story of two house-builders, one wise and the other foolish:

> *Therefore every one who hears these words of Mine, and acts upon them, may be compared to a wise man, who built his house upon the rock. And the rain descended, and the floods came, and the winds blew, and burst against that house; and yet it did not fall, for it had been founded upon the rock. Everyone who hears these words of Mine, and does not act upon them, will be like a foolish man, who built his house upon the sand. And the rain descended, and the floods came, and the winds blew, and burst against that house; and it fell —and great was its fall (Matthew 7:24–27).*

When the storm came, the house built on the rock remained standing, while the house built on the sand was washed away. Jesus' point is that His Word is the rock—the only solid foundation upon which we can build our lives. People all around us are building their lives on the shifting sand of human philosophy, false religion, and the passing riches of the world. It is no wonder that such a shaky foundation leaves them unprepared for the storm. Jesus assured us that if we build our lives on the solid foundation of His Word, we will never be destroyed when trouble comes our way, but will withstand every storm, no matter how fierce.

Basing your life on the sandy foundation of the principles, formulas, and doctrines of men will lead inevitably to ruin. On the other hand, establishing your life on the rock of Jesus Christ and His Word will enable you to stand firm against the storms of trouble, hardship, and adversity. Whatever your problem—a bad report from the doctor, getting fired, your spouse walking out, abuse, addiction—Jesus will get you through it.

Storms will come; they are inevitable. You cannot escape them, which is why you need to prepare for them now. Examine yourself carefully to make sure you are building your life on the right foundation— Jesus Christ. Nothing else will carry you safely into your future.

Once you stand up, act on your faith, and start to build, things will begin to change. People will begin to respect you and to treat you differently. As your self-esteem improves you will start to feel better about yourself. Your finances will begin to turn around. Opportunities you never dreamed of before will knock on your door. Never underestimate in your life the importance of the right foundation or the power of the Word of God.

Make Some Changes

Your circumstances will never change until you make up your mind to change them. God stands ready to help you, but He will do little without your willing and active involvement. Until you take concrete steps to build a better life, the future you dream of will remain only a dream.

What's holding you back? Are you tired of your dead-end job? Maybe it's time to go back to school and train for a better one. Have you thought about starting your own business? This may be the time.

Do you need to get rid of some bad attitudes or self-destructive habits? Are anger, resentment, and bitterness eating you alive? You may need to forgive someone before you can move forward.

If you sit back and wait for God to do it all, you will miss your destiny. Take action now, looking to the Lord for wisdom and guidance. Whether He has called you to build a business, build a ministry, go to school, become a teacher, or write a book, unless you prepare today, nothing will change tomorrow. Just because you have a calling on your life does not mean that it will automatically come to pass. You have to both prepare for and fight for your destiny. You have to step out of the debris of past failures and actively build for your future. Unless you bury your dead past, it will very likely bury you.

> *"Your circumstances will never change until you make up your mind to change them."*

The problem with building something is that it doesn't happen overnight. Anything worth building takes time. It takes time to build a television ministry. It takes time to build a business. It takes time to build a family. It takes time to get full of the Word of God. It takes time to build a prayer life. It takes time to learn how to lay hands on the sick. It takes time to plant seed in the kingdom of God and wait for a harvest. It takes time to overcome the sins and setbacks of the past. Although building may be a long process, don't wait around. Begin today. There is no better time than the present.

Change is risky, but little of significance in life is ever achieved without some risk. Once you decide to step out and make changes, you may face discouragement. Whatever else you do, hang in there. The Bible says not to lose heart in doing good because you will reap in due season. If God has told you to build, you'd better start sawing wood and hammering nails. Trust that in His time, God will work everything out. The risks of obeying God are nothing compared to the consequences of disobedience.

It's Time to Build for Your Future

Soar With the Eagles

Anyone who wants to become an exceptional person must spend time around exceptional people. We all tend to become like the people we hang around with. If you want to know what kind of person you really are, just take a look at your friends. Who are they? What are they doing? Where are they going in life? If they are losers, then you probably are too. If they are builders, then you probably are as well. The people you hang with are a pretty good indicator of who you are and where you will be a year from now, two years from now, or five years from now. As you look at your friends, ask yourself, "Do I really want to be where they are five years from now?"

Nothing will change until you decide to change. If you are serious about your future, you may need to change some of your friends. You need to walk with people who are going somewhere, people who will challenge you to strive harder to succeed. Being around challenging people will inspire you to find and bring out the greatest and best in yourself.

Building a better future and striving for excellence never come without a price. Your success will come only at the cost of a lot of time, energy, effort, planning, patience, sweat, tears, and most of all, *faith*. When God is working in your life, He will allow you to go through some storms in order to take you to a higher level. Developing the toughness and flexibility to weather the storms of life can make the difference between whether you become ordinary or extraordinary. Depending on your attitude and character, trouble will cause you either to quit or to become a builder. Which will it be?

Remember that trouble is one way that God prepares us for greatness. Trouble teaches us to lean on God rather than on ourselves. A life without storms or challenges is a life that is stagnant and near death. Storms are catalysts for change, which is why God allows us to go through them. He wants to bring some changes into our lives today so we will be ready for a brighter and better future tomorrow.

Stop running with the chickens and start soaring with the eagles. Don't worry about what other people say or think. Be a God-pleaser, not a people-pleaser. Get up, get on with your life, and start building for the future. You were born with a God-given assignment on your life and it is time to build. It doesn't matter if you were a crack baby or grew up in a foster home. It doesn't matter if your past is full of nothing but mistakes and failures. That was then, and this is now. God has a great purpose for your life and plans for your success.

Sometimes life gets hard and times get tough. You will get so tired and so discouraged that you will be ready to quit. Where do you find the strength to keep going and the courage to continue building? There is only one place: Jesus Christ. He is the Rock, the only sure and solid foundation for your life. When you rest in Him, He renews your strength. As the prophet Isaiah said, *"Those who wait for the LORD will gain new strength; they will mount up with wings like eagles, they will run and not get tired, they will walk and not become weary"* (Isaiah 40:31).

A life of sin and disobedience is a life built on the sand, a life with no future. Building on the solid foundation of Christ and His Word yields a life of righteousness with a future of unlimited possibilities. Sin will steal everything you have, but righteousness will strengthen you and build you up. Sin will leave you broke, but righteousness will cause you to prosper. Sin will tear your house down, but righteousness will build it up. Sin will destroy your relationships, but righteousness will strengthen them. Sin will block your progress, but righteousness will open the way for God to do a new thing in your life.

Get busy building your life firmly on Jesus Christ because, *"unless the LORD builds the house, they labor in vain who build it"* (Psalm 127:1). From start to finish, it is a journey of faith.

Chapter Eleven

FAITH JOURNEY

Once we make up our minds to leave our failed past behind and build toward a new and better future, we embark on a faith journey. Although the decision to embrace the future may be ours to make, our ultimate success depends on the Lord, and this is where faith comes in. Because our natural tendency as humans is to believe in what we can see, hear, smell, taste, and touch, we often have trouble placing our trust in someone we cannot perceive with our natural senses.

Nevertheless, that is the essence of faith. Paul said that as Christians we walk by faith, not by sight (see 2 Corinthians 5:7). Our physical senses can deceive us, and the apparent reality of our current circumstances often leaves us with a distorted picture of what is really happening in our lives. Sometimes when we are exercising faith and believing God for a certain thing, the opposite happens. Although it is only temporary, at the time it looks to us as though God has not answered our prayers.

Here is an example. Let's say you have been praying and believing God for an improvement in your finances when suddenly you get laid off at work. By all appearances, the loss of your job has made your situation worse. In reality it may be the prelude for something greater. Losing your job may be God's way of opening the door to a better job with better pay and better benefits, or even to starting your own business. God is always working on our behalf, but more often than not, He works behind the scenes. That is why it is important to walk by faith and not by sight.

Faith is believing with confidence for something even in the absence of visible evidence. As the writer of Hebrews says, *"Now faith is the assurance of things hoped for, the conviction of things not seen"* (Hebrews 11:1). Biblical faith means trusting in the Word of God as more sure and certain than anything that we can perceive with our human senses. Walking by faith is the *only* path to true and lasting success and prosperity. This is because the life of faith is the only lifestyle that pleases God: *"Without faith it is impossible to please Him, for he who comes to God must believe that He is, and that He is a rewarder of those who seek Him"* (Hebrews 11:6).

The enemy knows this, which is why he is always trying to steal our faith. He does not want us to please the Lord or to receive the rewards that come from faith. He does not want us to live a victorious life. Instead, he tries to get us to stop following the Lord by filling our minds with guilt and condemnation. He sows seeds of doubt and unbelief in our spirits in the hope that we will abandon our faith.

Make no mistake about it, hell has a strategy to steal everything you have—your faith, your joy, your peace, your love, your health, your prosperity, and your future. Satan wants to make you ineffective in the body of Christ. He will do everything he can to hold you in the past and make you believe that you are not going anywhere and never will. If he can convince you to believe his lies, he can rob you of your future. Faith is the antidote to his lies and the gateway to a glorious future in Christ that the devil cannot touch.

Walking by faith does have a price. Sometimes faith will take us into the fiery furnace or through the valley of the shadow of death. When we walk by faith we can expect pain, trials, tribulations, and unpleasant circumstances along the way. Don't forget that those troubles help toughen us and prepare us for greater things. Even more importantly, when we walk by faith we can expect the continual presence and power of the Lord with us.

True faith is grounded in the Word of God. A victorious life is established on the solid foundation of Jesus Christ. Faith is the framework upon which everything else is built. If you want to live in victory, you must walk by faith, determined to live by every word that proceeds out of the mouth of God. Paul said, *"Faith comes from hearing, and hearing by the word of Christ"* (Romans 10:17). Fill your mind and life with the Word of God in every possible way—read it, study it, meditate on it, memorize it, hear it preached and taught. As you do, the fruit of your hearing will be faith imparted into your heart.

> *"Walking by faith is the only path to true and lasting success and prosperity."*

Faith is a gift from God that comes through a personal relationship with Him through Jesus Christ. We do not receive faith by joining a church or a denomination. Faith comes by walking daily with the Lord, listening to Him, and thereby coming to know Him. Because our Lord is living and active, so must our faith be. There is no such thing as passive faith. Faith is always active, always moving, always pressing forward into the future. When we exercise our faith, it always takes us somewhere. It always transports us to places we have never been before.

Faith Always Takes You Somewhere

Faith is like a muscle—the more we exercise it, the stronger it becomes. On the other hand, if we neglect our faith, it will atrophy. One reason God allows us to go through hard times is because our faith grows and matures more quickly at such times than during easy times. When things are going well we have a tendency to stop depending on the Lord and start relying on our own wisdom, strength, or resources. Tough times reveal our weaknesses as well as His strengths, our inadequacy as well as His all-sufficiency. Hardships help us understand that without the Lord we are finished. Without Christ's presence and power we will never make it through the storms that come against us.

From the human standpoint, faith is risky because it involves trusting in the unknown. Reaching out to claim our destiny always involves an element of risk. It is easier to simply stay where we are. Viewed from God's perspective, however, faith carries no risk at all because God is faithful. We can trust Him with complete confidence.

When you truly walk by faith, you will learn to expect the unexpected and believe for the impossible. What you see and hear around you never tells the whole story. God can turn your situation around regardless of your track record. He can turn your failures into successes and your defeats into victories. Paul said that God *"is able to do exceeding abundantly beyond all that we ask or think, according to the power that works within us"* (Ephesians 3:20). That is why you cannot rely solely on what you think, hear, or see. Your senses may tell you, "I can't," but the Lord says, "*I* can." Faith means standing on the Word of God.

Faith and words work together. Our speech reflects our faith. Examine your own speech. What comes out of your mouth? When you are walking by faith, you will speak love, joy, peace, patience, trust, and confidence. Negative words and attitudes are a sure sign that you are *not* walking by faith. If you are judging your future prospects by your current circumstances, you are probably walking by sight. Unless you change your words and your outlook, you will end up negative, discouraged, and thoroughly defeated.

James 3:3 compares the words we speak to the bit in a horse's mouth, which the rider uses to control and guide it to the left or right. In the same way, your words will guide you either to faith or to doubt and unbelief. When you walk by faith, your words will express faith. Words are like seeds; they reproduce after their own kind, either positive or negative. Whether you bear positive or negative fruit in your life depends on what kind of seeds you sow.

Faith is a gift from God that always moves you onward and upward. It takes you from where you are to where God wants you to be. Faith lifts you from guilt to glory, from defeat to victory, and from sorrow to joy. Through faith you rise to become an overcomer in the world. First John 5:4 says, *"For whatever is born of God overcomes the world; and this is the victory that has overcome the world—our faith."* If you are born again, your faith gives you the ability to overcome all the darkness that comes against you. Whether it is sickness, poverty, low self-esteem, family problems, rejection, or any of the sins of your past, your faith in the Lord will help you overcome.

> *"Faith never backs up, never gives up, and never turns around."*

Let's face it, the devil will never leave us alone. Since that is so, we need to prepare ourselves to confront and overcome his attacks. If we were to rely on our own strength alone, we would have no hope. Fortunately, all the resources of heaven are available to us. Paul said, *"The weapons of our warfare are not of the flesh, but divinely powerful for the destruction of fortresses"* (2 Corinthians 10:4). Although he was talking about fortresses or strongholds of the mind, Paul's words still apply because most of Satan's attacks aim at our minds—our thoughts, perceptions, attitudes, and mental processes.

Next to the spiritual arsenal that we have in the Lord, Satan's weapons are ineffective: *" 'No weapon that is formed against you shall prosper; and every tongue that accuses you in judgment you will condemn. This is the heritage of the servants of the LORD, and their vindication is from Me,' declares the LORD"* (Isaiah 54:17). As long as we walk by faith and serve the Lord faithfully, the devil cannot win, no matter what he brings against us. God's promise for every faithful believer is that no disease, no amount of family trouble, no amount of financial trouble, no amount of difficulty of any kind shall prevail. In Christ we can rise above every challenge and defeat every foe.

Faith is the victory that overcomes the world. When we walk by faith we are always moving forward and always climbing higher. Faith never backs up, never gives up, and never turns around. By faith, we *"press on toward the goal for the prize of the upward call of God in Christ Jesus"* (Philippians 3:14).

Faith for the Impossible

Genuine faith in the Lord opens the door for the impossible to take place. He is the God of the impossible, the one who can make a way where there is no way. Even when everyone else fails you or walks away from you, God will never forsake you. If the bottom falls out of your life and you lose everything, He will still be there. No one can steal your faith, and nothing can separate you from the love of Christ. In *all* things you are more than a conqueror through Him who loves you and gave Himself for you.

When you trust in an infinite God, suddenly the impossible becomes possible. The doctors may have given up hope, but Jesus *is* your hope, and nothing is beyond His power. He can heal you when no one else can. You may be out of work, out of money, and out of ideas, but God is *Jehovah-Jireh*, your Provider, who knows your needs and takes care of them all. He can turn your poverty into plenty even when you have no idea where your next paycheck will come from.

God is big enough to bring down every mountain, straighten out every crooked path, and smooth over every rough place that we encounter on our faith journey. He can deliver us *from* the lion's den or protect us *in* the lion's den; He can deliver us *from* the fiery furnace or walk with us *through* the fiery furnace. When we walk by faith we can do all things through Christ who strengthens us (see Philippians 4:13).

Religion cannot give us this kind of faith. Neither can philosophy. It cannot be found in the things of the world or in the thoughts of men. Only God can impart faith. Overcoming faith is not found by sitting in Sunday school or watching Christian television. It does not come through the normal affairs of life when things are running smoothly. Faith to overcome grows when we hit a brick wall and have no one to turn to except the Lord. It grows when we face a crisis too big for us to handle that threatens to destroy us, only to see the Lord deliver us. Prevailing faith teaches us to say, even in the face of losing everything, "Lord, I trust You, and I know that with Your help I will overcome."

Faith Journey

The Good Fight of Faith

Faith that overcomes is a faith that has learned how to fight. We face many struggles in life, and perhaps the hardest of all is the struggle that Paul referred to as the *"good fight of faith"* (1 Timothy 6:12). One of the first things you will discover when you get serious about following the Lord is how serious the devil gets about stopping you. He will use every trick in the book to try to shake your faith, get you to deny God, tempt you to sin, consume you with guilt, lead you astray by false teaching, make you feel that you are going nowhere, and convince you that you are beyond redemption.

The devil is a very convincing and persuasive liar. He will lie about God, he will lie about you, he will lie about your friends, he will lie about anyone or anything if he thinks it will cause you to stop following the Lord. One of the hardest parts of fighting the good fight of faith is learning to stand firm against Satan's onslaught and refusing to believe his lies. If ever you do fall for one, then the devil has won ninety percent of the battle.

Unlike conventional warfare, the good fight of faith is a spiritual battle requiring spiritual weapons and unconventional tactics. Although there are many times when the good fight requires us to go on the offensive, advancing boldly under the banner of the Cross in the power of the Holy Spirit, even more often it calls for us to stand fast and let the Lord fight the battle for us.

That is exactly what happened with the Israelites at the Red Sea. As Pharaoh's army drew near and the people began to panic, Moses cried out, *"Do not fear! Stand by and see the salvation of the LORD which He will accomplish for you today; for the Egyptians whom you have seen today, you will never see them again forever. The LORD will fight for you while you keep silent"* (Exodus 14:13–14). All the Israelites had to do was believe, stand fast, and watch as God delivered them.

Standing and waiting is hard because it requires more faith than taking action does. We all have a tendency to trust in our own strength or wits or feel that it is up to us to get ourselves out of a tight spot. When the enemy is breathing down our neck it is hard to simply cast our cares on the Lord without trying to defend ourselves. Daniel had the faith in God not to resist when he was thrown into the lion's den, and God delivered him safely. In faith, Shadrach, Meshach, and Abednego refused to worship the king's idol, even though it meant being thrown into a fiery furnace. The Lord was with them in the fire, however, and they emerged unharmed. When it comes to the good fight of faith, sometimes the best strategy is simply to stand.

God does not leave us to stand defenseless. He equips us with a formidable arsenal of weapons for the fight. Paul called it the "armor of God":

Therefore, take up the full armor of God, that you may be able to resist in the evil day, and having done everything, to stand firm. Stand firm therefore, having girded your loins with truth, and having put on the breastplate of righteousness, and having shod your feet with the preparation of the gospel of peace; in addition to all, taking up the shield of faith with which you will be able to extinguish all the flaming missiles of the evil one. And take the helmet of salvation, and the sword of the Spirit, which is the word of God. With all prayer and petition pray at all times in the Spirit, and with this in view, be on the alert with all perseverance and petition for all the saints (Ephesians 6:14–18).

Truth, righteousness, peace, faith, salvation, the Holy Spirit, the Word of God, and prayer—against weapons like these, the devil doesn't stand a chance!

Your faith journey should lead you to the point where you can face down the enemy and say, "You can threaten me all you want. You can throw me into the fire. You can talk about me. You can even take everything I own, but you cannot defeat me. You may land a few punches, but you will never knock me down for the count. I will still be standing because I trust in the Lord, and He will restore everything you have taken. I may have been down, but I'm not out. My best days are still ahead."

The wonderful thing about walking by faith is that you do not have to worry about your life or where you are going. God is in charge and He will take you where He wants you to be. At times the ride may be a little bumpy and have some dangerous curves, but God has ordered your steps. Whatever you may be going through now is only temporary. Your faith in the Lord will always lead you onward and upward, and eventually, God will cause you to triumph.

All that God asks is that you be willing to let go of your hurts, your regrets, your sense of failure, and all the other baggage of your past, and walk with Him by faith. People who live by faith learn to walk in love, and their hurts begin to heal and miracles begin to happen in their lives.

God is ready to take you to a new place of blessing, but He cannot do so until you are ready to leave your past behind and walk forward by faith. Remember that faith is believing God for the best even when you cannot see it right now. God *will* answer your prayers. His answer may not come today, but if you are walking by faith, that won't matter. Faith will teach you to say, "I do not need the answer today. I know that in the Lord's good time the answer will come, and that is enough."

DON'T JUDGE MY FUTURE BY MY PAST

Chapter Twelve

BE ANXIOUS FOR NOTHING

W alking by faith is the only way to live securely and confidently. You see, so often life does not always work out the way we planned. No matter how careful we are, we cannot prepare for everything. Sometimes life takes sudden unexpected and difficult turns, and if we lose control on the curves, we can end up bruised and bleeding by the side of the road. Whether self-inflicted or the result of what others have done to us, the hard knocks of life can leave us hurting for a long time.

Every day we encounter thousands of things we could worry about if we wanted to: bad credit, a troubled marriage, rebellious children, financial problems, job security, terrorist attacks, illness, accidents, violent crime, nuclear war, you name it. Mental institutions and hospital psychiatric wards across the country are filled with people who are unable to cope with the anxieties of daily life.

Although life's uncertainties stir up anxiety in the minds of many people, we who know the Lord should be free of worry because our lives are secure in Him. Jesus said, *"Let not your heart be troubled; believe in God, believe also in Me"* (John 14:1). The apostle Peter offered this counsel: *"Humble yourselves, therefore, under the mighty hand of God, that He may exalt you at the proper time, casting all your anxiety upon Him, because He cares for you"* (1 Peter 5:6–7). Humble trust in the Lord is the antidote for anxiety.

> *"Humble trust in the Lord is the antidote for anxiety."*

Now that we are born again, we are supposed to cast all of our cares on the Lord and let Him take care of them. His shoulders are big enough to carry the burdens of life that we cannot bear. When we allow ourselves to worry or be anxious, we make ourselves vulnerable to fear. Once fear has a foothold in our minds, it quickly takes control and colors the way we look at everything. We worry about the past, fret over the present, and dread the future. With fear in charge, we become obsessed with what other people think of us and spend all our energy and effort trying to please them. Fear distorts our perception so that we see neither ourselves nor other people clearly. Most of all, however, we end up with an unclear or incorrect perception of God.

Firm faith in the Lord will drive away fear. There is no room for fear in a life totally surrendered to Christ and filled with His love: *"For God has not given us a spirit of timidity, but of power and love and discipline"* (2 Timothy 1:7); *"There is no fear in love; but perfect love casts out fear"* (1 John 4:18).

Don't allow other people's opinions of you (or your *perception* of their opinions) to steal your future. God's opinion is the only one that matters. Set yourself on becoming a God-pleaser rather than a people pleaser. Once you learn to banish fear through faith, you can fully exercise the spirit of *"power and love and discipline"* that God gave you to become all that He wants you to be and to claim the future He has planned for you.

Pray Without Ceasing

Worry is one of the greatest enemies we face in life. Deadly to our faith and dangerous to our overall health, unrestrained worry contributes to depression, ulcers, heart disease, and many other mental, emotional, and physical illnesses. Worry is like a rocking chair or a treadmill: It gives us something to do but we never go anywhere. When we worry, we expend a great deal of time and energy with nothing to show for our efforts. What's even worse is that most of the time the things we worry about either never happen or turn out to be much less serious than we imagined. In the end, all our anxiety comes to no purpose.

We try to hold on to things that we ought to let go of. We try to protect our children, but there is only so much that we can do. We lie awake at night worrying about things over which we have no control. No matter how hard we try to hold on, we feel those things that are most important to us slipping from our grasp. The worries of life consume us so completely that we cannot smile anymore. Going to church no longer holds any pleasure or joy for us because anxiety has choked out the Word of God from our hearts. We are so stressed out that we cannot eat, sleep, or enjoy life.

Don't waste your time worrying about the past. There is nothing you can do to change it. Worrying about the future makes no sense either because you are reading the worst into events that have not even occurred yet. When you worry about the present, you rob yourself of the time and opportunity to think and prepare constructively for the future. Worry will steal your peace, your joy, your assurance of God's love for you. It also will take away your ability to fully love others and to experience their love in return. Given long enough, worry will sap your strength and your faith and will steal the Word of God out of your heart.

How do we guard against worry? What can we do to keep anxiety from overtaking us and controlling our lives? Paul provided the answer when he wrote, *"Be anxious for nothing, but in everything by prayer and supplication with thanksgiving let your requests be made known to God. And the peace of God, which surpasses all comprehension, shall guard your hearts and your minds in Christ Jesus"* (Philippians 4:6–7). The contrast could not be any sharper: We are to be anxious for *nothing*, but pray in *everything*. This is the same idea as Peter's instruction to cast all our cares upon the Lord.

In another place, Paul stated it even more succinctly: *"Pray without ceasing"* (1 Thessalonians 5:17).

Prayer is our most potent weapon against worry and anxiety. Whenever these things threaten, our best defense is to pray over everything and leave the results in God's hands. Nothing can take the place of prayer. Paul never said we should clap without ceasing, or shout without ceasing, or sing without ceasing, or even read God's Word without ceasing. He said we should *pray* without ceasing. Prayer aligns our hearts and attitudes with God and opens the windows of heaven, enabling Him to fill us with His power and pour out His blessings on us.

> *"Prayer is our most potent weapon against worry and anxiety."*

The Lord has promised that if we give our worries to Him, He will take care of us. Praying in faith with thanksgiving defuses anxiety and fills us with a divine peace that is incomprehensible by human wisdom and that guards our hearts and minds in Christ. Anxiety stems from our tendency to depend too much on the temporary things of the world that are passing away. God's peace defies human logic because it can fill our hearts even when everything around us seems to be falling apart. It is an unshakable peace because it is established on the unchanging nature and character of God.

All of us experience times when the pressures and unknowns of life weigh us down. We are particularly prone to worry during times of illness, fatigue, or unexpected setbacks. These are the times when we need to be especially careful. No matter the circumstance, whenever or wherever anxiety rises up, God's answer is for us to pray. When we pray without ceasing, we have no time for worry. We simply release the problem or situation to the Lord and trust Him to take care of it.

There is something about prayer that keeps our hearts and minds focused on Christ Jesus. It is hard to explain, particularly to someone who has never experienced it, but when we pray and release our anxieties to the Lord, a peace comes upon us that cannot be shaken, no matter how severe the storm. God's peace can calm even the most troubled soul.

Are you weighed down with worry and doubt? Let them go. As long as you insist on worrying, there is little God can do for you. There is even less that you can do for yourself. You will never overcome the worries of life until you learn to confess that nothing is impossible with God (see Luke 1:37) and that you can do all things in Christ who is your strength (see Philippians 4:13).

The only way you can live without worry is by learning to pray about everything, releasing your past to the Lord, and trusting Him completely for your future. Remember the promise from Proverbs: *"Trust in the LORD with all your heart, and do not lean on your own understanding. In all your ways acknowledge Him, and He will make your paths straight"* (Proverbs 3:5–6).

Even if your whole world falls apart, even if you lose everything you have, keep the faith and pray. Trust that God has a purpose for everything that happens in your life and that He will restore you in His time. You may not understand what is going on, but your responsibility is to pray and not worry. Worrying changes nothing, but prayer changes everything. James said, *"The effective prayer of a righteous man can accomplish much"* (James 5:16). The context of James' words is praying for healing, but they apply equally to every area of need or anxiety in life. Whatever your anxiety, let go of it and trust the Lord.

Don't Worry About Daily Needs

One of Satan's favorite tactics is to convince us that there are some things too small or insignificant for us to "bother" God with. He fills our minds with the lie that God is too busy to concern Himself with the mundane issues of our daily lives. In fact, the exact opposite is true. Concern for daily needs is one of the things Jesus specifically identified as a legitimate object of prayer: *"Give us this day our daily bread"* (Matthew 6:11). He *wants* us to pray to Him for the provision of our daily needs.

God's daily provision is not limited to food and water. He wants us to trust Him to provide *everything* we need because that is what a life of faith is all about. A little later in the sixth chapter of Matthew, Jesus assures us that just as God takes care of the birds of the air and the lilies of the field, He will also take care of us. This is why we should never worry about the future. God gives us today what we need for today, and tomorrow is in His hands. What He did today He will do tomorrow, because He is faithful.

With this in mind, consider Jesus' words:

> *Do not be anxious then, saying, "What shall we eat?" or "What will we drink?" or "With what shall we clothe our-selves?" For all these things the Gentiles eagerly seek; for your heavenly Father knows that you need all these things. But seek first His kingdom and His righteousness; and all these things shall be added to you. Therefore do not be anxious for tomorrow; for tomorrow will care for itself. Each day has enough trouble of its own* (Matthew 6:31–34).

God has a plan for your life and is moving you toward your future. Don't be anxious about your daily circumstances because He has promised to take care of you. In the words of Paul, *"My God shall supply all your needs according to His riches in glory in Christ Jesus"* (Philippians 4:19).

All Things Work Together for Good

The devil wants to steal your peace of mind by getting you to fret over your past failures and worry about your present circumstances. That is when you most need to remember that the Lord is walking with you through the valley, whether it is the valley of despair, the valley of dry bones, or the valley of the shadow of death. If God is sovereign, He is in charge of your life and you can stop worrying. No matter how many arrows the enemy shoots at you, no matter what kinds of storms life slams you with, the Lord will turn them to your good in His time and in His way. He will change your adversities into assets and your banes into blessings because, *"We know that God causes all things to work together for good to those who love God, to those who are called according to His purpose"* (Romans 8:28).

Before you came to the Lord, you were dead in your trespasses and sins (see Ephesians 2:1). You were a slave to your sinful nature, separated from God and under His judgment because of your sin. The moment you gave your life to Christ, your entire situation changed. Christ brought you from slavery to freedom, from guilt to forgiveness, and from death to life. He is committed to your good and your future. If you love the Lord, it does not matter what you have gone through or what you are going through now. He will turn it to your good.

> *"God is committed to your good and your future."*

Your troubles will not last forever, and all things will eventually work for your benefit and God's glory. You may be pressed in on every side, but the pressure will make you better and stronger. If the stress of your situation tempts you to throw in the towel, remember Paul's encouragement to *"not lose heart in doing good, for in due time we shall reap if we do not grow weary"* (Galatians 6:9).

Worry is wearisome; it tires us out and saps our spirit. Faith coupled with regular prayer opens the channels through which God's refreshing waters of joy, peace, encouragement, hope, and confidence can flow. Although sometimes we have little control over what happens to us, we do have control over our attitude and our response to what happens.

None of the worries and hardships of life will ever get you down as long as you remember that God is working all things together for your good. The key to your success in dealing with anxiety is to *love God with all your heart.* This means giving your life to Him in faith, committing yourself to serve Him, and seeking to honor Him in everything you do, striving always to live a life free of sin.

Once you make such a commitment, nothing can stop you from putting your past behind you and entering your promised land of abundant living in Christ Jesus. Cast all your cares on the Lord and

He will work all things together for your good. The more you learn to trust and pray, the more worry and anxiety will melt away and fade into the past.

We serve a God who never sleeps or slumbers. Because He is always awake, we can sleep in peace and without fear, safe in His arms. The Lord has called us by name and we are His. He will be with us when we pass through the fire and we will not be burned. No matter what we go through, He is with us, and when we are with Him, we are safe. Psalm 91 contains a wonderful promise: *"He who dwells in the shelter of the Most High will abide in the shadow of the Almighty. I will say to the LORD, 'My refuge and my fortress, my God, in whom I trust!' "* (Psalm 91:1–2)

Almighty God, the Most High, our refuge and fortress and the God in whom we trust, is bigger than all our problems. He is the great miracle worker who works all things together for our good. The Lord can overcome all the sin and failure of our past and all the worry and anxiety of our present, and open up before us a future more brilliant than anything we could possibly imagine.

With God nothing is impossible. That is why you can leave your past and start over no matter who you are, where you've been, or what you've done. He is the God of second, third, fourth, fifth, and even tenth chances. What you, unable to see past your own failures, could not do, God did. He looked *beyond* your faults to the future He had planned for you from before the foundation of the world. Then He went to work to bring you into it.

Chapter Thirteen

HE LOOKED BEYOND YOUR FAULTS

God has always had a plan for us. In the beginning, God created man for continual fellowship with Him and to exercise dominion over the created realm. Adam and Eve's sin in the Garden of Eden broke that fellowship and disrupted their dominion rule. They were separated from God as well as from their intended destiny.

As descendants of Adam and Eve, we all inherited their sinful nature. Like them, we too were separated from God and from His original plan. The theme of the entire Bible is the working out of God's plan to bring us back into relationship with Himself and to restore all that we lost because of the fall.

In the second chapter of Ephesians, Paul said that we were dead in our trespasses and sins and walked according to the way of the world, freely indulging the lusts of our flesh and the desires of our minds. By nature we were *"children of wrath"* (Ephesians 2:3), meaning that because of our sin, we were under God's holy and righteous judgment and condemnation. On our own we were helpless and hopeless, guilty and with no defense before the Lord.

Fortunately for us, God took action when we could not:

But God, being rich in mercy, because of His great love with which He loved us, even when we were dead in our transgressions, made us alive together with Christ (by grace you have been saved), and raised us up with Him, and seated us with Him in the heavenly places, in Christ Jesus, in order that in the ages to come He might show the surpassing riches of His grace in kindness toward us in Christ Jesus (Ephesians 2:4–7).

God saved us by His grace and showered us with His love and His *mercy*. Grace is God's unmerited favor—the favor He extended to us even when we did not deserve it. Love is the very nature of God. Mercy is the quality of showing leniency toward the undeserving. None of us deserved either God's favor or His mercy, yet He gave us both. The blood Jesus shed on the cross made our forgiveness possible. His death paid the penalty for our sin. God's grace forgives us, but His mercy spares us. In Christ, the grace of God regards us as though we had never sinned, while His mercy cancels the punishment that is our due.

> *"God's grace forgives us, but His mercy spares us."*

What more could God do to show us what He thinks of us? He poured out His grace and mercy on us undeserving sinners and made us alive in Christ. By so doing, He proved that He is not mad at us. He loves us with an infinite love and wants to bless us. God's lovingkindness (mercy) is everlasting. As the psalmist says, this is reason enough to be thankful:

Give thanks to the LORD, for He is good; for His lovingkindness is everlasting. Give thanks to the God of gods, for His lovingkindness is everlasting. Give thanks to the Lord of lords, for His lovingkindness is everlasting (Psalm 136:1–3).

When was the last time you thanked the Lord for His goodness and mercy toward you? Think about all He has done in your life. God's mercy is greater than your sin, greater than your guilt, greater than any of your failures, and greater than the biggest mistakes you have ever made. His mercy is greater than all the negative baggage of your past. Nothing you have ever done or ever will do is beyond the reach of the mercy of God. No matter what baggage you carry or what hurts you bear, no matter how much despair or sorrow fill your days, God's mercy will help you to heal and to experience His joy. Mercy gives you what you need, not what you deserve. It is like standing before your Father expecting a stern rebuke, only to receive a warm embrace instead.

Mercy Is God's Prerogative

Many times God's actions toward us or toward others seem to defy human logic. This should not surprise us since we have limited understanding while God is limitless. Besides, God does not do things the way we do. He makes this clear in His Word: " *'For My thoughts are not your thoughts, neither are your ways My ways,' declares the LORD. 'For as the heavens are higher than the earth, so are My ways higher than your ways, and My thoughts than your thoughts' "* (Isaiah 55:8–9). It would do us well to keep this in mind any time we are tempted to make value judgments about other people.

It is our nature, even as believers, to classify people with regard to how useful we think they are to God. Despite our own experiences, we often judge people by their past, their appearance, their education or lack thereof, or by whether or not they have any "marketable" skills. We even judge how "spiritual" we think they are, particularly compared to ourselves.

Once we ourselves are safely in the kingdom of God, it is easy to forget where we came from. We can easily fall into the trap of strutting our holiness in front of others, as if our position with God was due to our own merit. The *only* reason we are forgiven and in a right relationship with the Lord is because of *His* grace and mercy. Before we judge or classify others, we need to remember that *we all* have a limp of one kind or another. All of us have some things in our past that we are not proud of. None of us has the right to boast of our merit before God.

Mercy is God's prerogative. We have no right to tell God who He can or cannot use. Only God can turn weakness into strength or failure into greatness. Who else but God can take someone who has a horrible past and turn him around? God will always surprise us in His choice of people. Every now and then He will pull an old treasure out of the junk pile.

God never calls perfect people. First of all, there are none. Second, He is specifically after sinful, unrighteous, and imperfect people. Jesus said, *"It is not those who are healthy who need a physician, but those who are sick; I did not come to call the righteous, but sinners"* (Mark 2:17). The Lord is not looking for superstars, but for people who are willing to humble themselves.

God's mercies are new every morning. Abraham was an idolater, yet God made him the father of a nation holy to Himself. Moses was a murderer, yet God used him to deliver that same nation from slavery in Egypt. Rahab was a harlot, yet God used her to help the Israelites overthrow Jericho, their first conquest in the promised land. David was an adulterer and a murderer, but by God's mercy became Israel's greatest king. Peter denied Christ three times, but God's mercy picked him up and restored him. Paul savagely persecuted the followers of Christ, but through the mercy of God became Christ's apostle to the Gentiles.

If God could use people like these, then there is plenty of hope for you. No matter who you are or what you have done, if you humble yourself, repent, and turn to the Lord, He will look beyond your past, beyond what you *appear* to be, and say, "You are the righteousness of God."

The devil will try to convince you that you have messed up too badly for God to use. He may even try to make you believe that you have committed the unpardonable sin and are beyond God's forgiveness. The devil is a liar. Don't believe a word he says.

He Looked Beyond Your Faults

Now that you have given your life to Christ, God does not hold anything against you. Nothing you can do will ever make God turn His back on you. Even when it looks like you won't make it, God's mercy will be there to pick you up and get you going again. God knows all about you and loves you anyway. He wants you to walk in fellowship with Him.

The Quality of God's Mercy

Mercy is for the guilty. If you were falsely accused or wronged in some way, you would want justice, not mercy. What if you were guilty? Wouldn't you want mercy even though you deserved justice? Seeking mercy requires two things: an awareness of your guilt and the humility of spirit to ask for it. Jesus illustrated this one day with a parable about a Pharisee and a tax collector.

> *Two men went up into the temple to pray, one a Pharisee and the other a tax collector. The Pharisee stood and was praying this to himself: "God, I thank Thee that I am not like other people: swindlers, unjust, adulterers, or even like this tax-gatherer. I fast twice a week; I pay tithes of all that I get." But the tax-gatherer, standing some distance away, was even unwilling to lift up his eyes to heaven, but was beating his breast, saying, "God, be merciful to me, the sinner!" I tell you, this man went to his house justified rather than the other; for every one who exalts himself will be humbled, but he who humbles himself shall be exalted* (Luke 18:10–14).

In his pride, the Pharisee did not recognize his need for God's forgiveness and mercy, so he received none. The tax collector, however, so overcome by his guilt that he could not even look toward heaven, simply prayed the only prayer that any of us as sinners could pray: *"God, be merciful to me, the sinner!"* God heard his prayer, accepted his repentance, and the tax collector went home knowing in his heart the peace and reality of God's mercy.

God is not mad at you. He loves you so much that He sent His only Son to die for your sins so that you could be restored to fellowship and a right relationship with Him. He is the God of second, third, fourth, and fifth chances. Even when no one else wanted you, God did. Even when everyone else had written you off, God picked you up and turned you around. Think about it—if it wasn't for the Lord on your side, where would you be today?

The devil will try to hold your sins and guilt over you to keep you enslaved to your past. When you came to Christ, you cast all your sins on Him, and He took them far away from you: *"As far as the east is from the west, so far has He removed our transgressions from us"* (Psalm 103:12).

> *"If it wasn't for the Lord on your side, where would you be today?"*

Without the mercy of God, you would be lost and without hope. What has God rescued you from? An abusive relationship? Depression? Suicidal tendencies? Did He preserve you through a divorce? Did He heal you of a heart attack or, perhaps, cancer? You may be alive today only because God's mercy brought you safely through the storm. When you were at the end of your strength, mercy stepped in and gave you new strength that was beyond your own.

God is faithful. His love and mercy never fail: *"The LORD'S lovingkindnesses indeed never cease, for His compassions never fail. They are new every morning; great is Thy faithfulness"* (Lamentations 3:22–23). God has a plan for your life that nothing can defeat. Even if you have failed God more times than you can count, His mercies are new every morning, and you can start over. There is no way you could ever deserve God's mercy—none of us could—but don't worry about that. By its very nature, mercy is reserved for the undeserving. That's what makes it mercy.

The Lord is good and His mercy endures forever. He is better to us than we are to ourselves. God is for us and His loyalty for us will never change. Friends or family may give up on us, but God never will. We are special to the Lord. If He was not on our side, the enemy would have destroyed us long ago. Because of God's mercy, no weapon of the enemy that is fashioned against us will stand. In Christ and His blood we have the victory.

He Looked Beyond Your Faults

God knows how weak we are, so His goodness and mercy stand behind us and uplift us at all times. David wrote, *"Surely goodness and lovingkindness will follow me all the days of my life, and I will dwell in the house of the LORD forever"* (Psalm 23:6). What a powerful promise! God's goodness and mercy follow us wherever we go. How can we lose?

Chosen to Be Blessed

As children of God, we have certain rights and privileges. Healing belongs to us. Prosperity and fruitfulness belong to us. Authority over the powers of darkness belongs to us. All these things and more are ours in Christ. God is rooting for us. He wants to see us win in every adverse situation we face.

The Lord promised that if we would diligently obey Him and put Him first, He would command His blessings upon us. God has chosen you to be blessed. That means that you do not have to settle for living on "Barely-Get-Along Street" anymore. Your heavenly Father desires your success and has the power to bring it to pass.

Once, when the great Renaissance sculptor Michelangelo bought a piece of marble that had terrible flaws in it, he was asked what he was going to do with it. He replied, "I see an angel locked up in the marble." That is the way God looks at you. He gazes beyond the flaws and imperfections that others see to the greatness deep inside you that cries to be released. God created you in His own image, and He does not make junk.

As believers, we are the chosen of God and the blessed of God, and the enemy cannot do anything about it. When Jesus gave His life, He was a seed planted in the ground. That seed has now come back in a bountiful harvest. The earth is filled with the sons and daughters of God, and the devil has no power to stop us.

Consider what the Lord has done for you. You were dead in your trespasses and sins and on your way to hell when He reached down, saved you from your sin, and made you a child in His holy and loving family. Washing away your past once and for all, He gave you a new beginning that guarantees you a bright hope and a brilliant future.

133

Remember our illustration about plant grafting? Anytime two plants are grafted together, a hole is cut in the side of one plant, and the other plant is fused into it. A wound is cut into the side of one plant so that the two plants can grow together. In the same way—figuratively speaking—our Lord Jesus Christ was wounded so that we could be grafted into the family of God: *"But He was pierced through for our transgressions, He was crushed for our iniquities; the chastening for our well-being fell upon Him, and by His scourging we are healed"* (Isaiah 53:5).

Whether you realize it or not, as a son or daughter of God, you have the right to walk in health, the right to live in peace, the right to live in prosperity, and the right to walk to the front of the line. It is time for you to acknowledge that you are not a second-class citizen in God's kingdom. The kingdom of God has no second-class citizens. Stop living beneath your privileges. With His blood, Jesus bought you the right to enter the kingdom of God with all its wealth, riches, resources, power, and blessings. It is yours and you are His not because you deserve it but because of His great mercy.

You are a new creature in Christ. He lifted the burden of your sin and carried it away. Your past has been washed away and your future in Christ Jesus is assured. God's mercy never fails, and He has chosen you as one of His children. No longer do you have to live in the bankrupt past. Now you have a new heritage, a new inheritance in the Lord. You are a child of the King and an heir to His kingdom. All His promises are yours. It is time to claim your rightful inheritance.

Chapter Fourteen

CLAIM YOUR INHERITANCE

❦

It is a great feeling to know that when the grace, love, and mercy of God covers you, neither you nor anyone else can judge your future by your past. Because you belong to Christ, your past is behind you and your future is assured. The more you understand who you really are in Christ Jesus, the less hold your past will have on you.

Before you were saved, you were in bondage, a slave to your sin. Christ set you free, not simply to the freedom of forgiven sin but also to the freedom that comes with being a member of God's family. John 1:12 says that all who receive Christ and believe in His name receive the right to become children of God. In his letter to the Romans, Paul got even more specific: *"For all who are being led by the Spirit of God, these are sons of God. For you have not received a spirit of slavery leading to fear again, but you have received a spirit of adoption as sons by which we cry out, 'Abba! Father!' "* (Romans 8:14–15)

By His grace, mercy, and sovereign choice, God has adopted you into His family. You are God's son or daughter, one of His chosen, and He has given you a glorious future with Him. It does not matter what happened before or what you used to be. As a child of God, your past has no bearing on your future. God looked beyond your faults and chose you to belong to Him.

Romans 8:15 says that God has given you a *"spirit of adoption."* When you were born again, you received the Holy Spirit as a permanent resident in your heart. He is the seal of God's ownership of you. The Holy Spirit is the one who enables you to cry out, "Abba, Father," which literally means that you are so close to God that you can call Him "Daddy." The Spirit in you assures you that "Daddy" loves you and is not mad at you.

One of the great tragedies of life is that there are so many unwanted and unloved children in the world. Some parents abandon, neglect, or abuse their children. Others never give their children a real chance at life because they abort them in the womb.

Adoption is different. Parents do not adopt unless they really want a child. In most cases they can examine a child's history— health, temperament, imperfections, physical characteristics, etc.— before making a final decision. Depending on their findings, they may choose to reject the child.

Unlike human adoption, God does not set standards of acceptance and rejection. When He wanted to fill His kingdom with His children, He looked at us with all our imperfections and still decided to adopt us. He looked beyond our faults and saw our needs. Knowing everything about our past, He chose us anyway. When we were orphans and homeless because of our sin, God adopted us and made us His own.

You are a child of God not because you chose Him but because He chose you. Jesus said, *"No longer do I call you slaves...but I have called you friends...You did not choose Me, but I chose you..."* (John 15:15–16). The Lord reached down, plucked you out of the dark alleys of sin, and brought you into His palace where He cleaned you up and adopted you into His family. He gave you His name when you had no name. He brought you out of your past and now wants to take you into a new and glorious future.

You may be wondering, "How do I *know* God loves me and wants me? What if He doesn't?" Depending on your past and how you were taught, you may have trouble feeling confident about God's love for you. I know I did once. Overcoming fear, guilt, and shame about the past is not always easy. If you were raised to see God as a harsh judge just waiting to pounce on you, it may be hard to view Him as a loving Father.

Think about it. If God did not love you, would He have sent His Son to die for you? Would He have adopted you if He did not want you? How do you know God loves you? Because of Jesus, who died that you might live. Because of His promise never to leave you or forsake you. Because He lifted you up when you were down. Because He stayed by your side when everyone else abandoned you.

God loves you with unconditional love. As His adopted child, you have no reason to fear Him. *"There is no fear in love; but perfect love casts out fear"* (1 John 4:18). Although the Bible says to "fear" God in the sense of showing Him reverence, awe, and respect, as a loved and adopted child of God, you have no reason to be afraid of your heavenly Father. He loves you, adopted you into His family, and made you an heir to His kingdom. This means that He has an inheritance prepared for you, an inheritance that is yours for the claiming.

Joint Heirs With Christ

Under the old covenant, the firstborn son was the primary heir of the family, inheriting two thirds of the estate. Other children received lesser amounts. The new covenant in Christ makes all of God's children equal heirs. Whether we are male or female, we all are sons of inheritance. As God's adopted children, we are heirs to all His promises and all His riches. Paul made this clear when he wrote, *"The Spirit Himself bears witness with our spirit that we are children of God, and if children, heirs also, heirs of God and fellow-heirs with Christ, if indeed we suffer with Him in order that we may also be glorified with Him"* (Romans 8:16–17). As joint heirs with Jesus, we share in His inheritance. Whatever belongs to Jesus also belongs to us.

In Galatians 2:20, Paul said that it is not we who live but Christ who lives in us. In Christ, you are no longer a slave to your past or to the sins that used to bind you. You are a joint heir with the King of kings and Lord of lords. It does not matter what your family background is—your family "pedigree"—for in Christ you have received the spirit of adoption. Where you came from is of no importance because your roots are now in Jesus Christ. What does it matter if you were born on the "wrong side of the tracks"? Now you have a rich family heritage in Christ.

As a child of God, you are a brother or sister to every other believer. Together we make up a royal priesthood and a holy nation. We are children of the King and citizens of His eternal kingdom. The blood of Jesus has made us into one holy race: the saints of God. Although we may have many different skin colors, we all look the same when covered in the blood of Jesus. Regardless of our ethnic or cultural background, in Christ we are members of the same family.

> *"We all look the same when covered in the blood of Jesus."*

In the Spirit of Christ, there is no reason why people of all races and colors cannot worship God together. Nothing should prevent believers of different backgrounds and cultures from loving, respecting, and appreciating one another. All this is possible because we have been adopted into God's family and have a new heritage in Jesus Christ.

As believers in Christ we are the spiritual seed of Abraham. God promised Abraham that his descendants—his "seed"—would become a great nation and would possess a land that He would give them. His promises include us. Because we are children of God and Abraham's seed, we are sons of inheritance. Just as He commanded the Israelites of old, God is telling us today to "go in and possess the land."

To "possess the land" means to go after the things that God says you can have. Go after that better job or more promising career, for God says it's yours. Go after your healing, for God says it's yours. Go after that piece of property or that house property, for God says it's yours. Go after a good family or a good relationship, for God says they are yours.

We are sons of inheritance, not because we deserve to be, but because He adopted us into His family when we made Jesus Lord of our lives. Whatever belongs to Jesus now belongs to us also because we are joint heirs with Him. Jesus is the heir, but we are the joint heirs. He did the work, but we benefit equally from His labor. He is the firstborn Son and our Elder Brother, and what's His is ours.

The Rights of the Sons

Before you can claim what is rightfully yours, you have to know that you are a son and that you are entitled to an inheritance. God has already given it to you. It is yours; He has set it out in His will. Daddy has already left you an inheritance, but how can you claim it if you don't know it's there and if you don't know it's yours? You may be living like a slave, unaware of the riches that belong to you. If you have ever dreamed of being wealthy, don't worry; as a joint heir with Christ, you already are! You are an heir to the kingdom of God.

God says that when we go into our promised land, His blessings belong to us. Listen to what Moses told the Israelites:

> Then it shall come about when the LORD your God brings you into the land which He swore to your fathers, Abraham, Isaac and Jacob, to give you, great and splendid cities which you did not build, and houses full of all good things which you did not fill, and hewn cisterns which you did not dig, vineyards and olive trees which you did not plant, and you shall eat and be satisfied (Deuteronomy 6:10–11).

God was telling them, "Because you are My children and I love you, I will give you cities you did not build, crops you did not grow, fruit trees you did not plant, cisterns you did not dig, and cattle you did not raise." In other words, He was going to bless them with things they had not worked for and did not deserve.

Our Father acts on behalf of His children *because* they are His children. He blesses us because we belong to Him. Even though we cannot earn God's blessings, there are conditions for receiving them. First, we have to know we are children, and therefore entitled. Second, we must be walking, living, and acting like His children. Just as God is quick to bless us when we obey Him, He withholds His blessings when we disobey.

Once you know who you are as a child of God and joint heir with Christ and are walking in obedience to His Word, God will begin doing things in your life. He will bless you in things and ways that you don't deserve. People will give you things and won't know why. Even people who don't like you will help you because you are a son. God will give you favor with them because He upholds His children.

> **"You cannot begin to imagine all that God has planned for you!"**

Because you are a son of inheritance, God will bring things into your life that would come no other way. Somehow, the chance will open up to buy that house you have always dreamed of but thought was way too good for you, and it will become yours. Someone unexpectedly will help you get the down payment you know you don't have. Paul wrote, *"Eye has not seen and ear has not heard, and which have not entered the heart of man, all that God has prepared for those who love Him"* (1 Corinthians 2:9). You cannot begin to imagine all that God has planned for you!

If you are trying to serve the Lord faithfully, His blessings will fall on you. If your parents were faithful servants of the Lord, He will pass on to you the blessings that came to them. Deuteronomy 7:9 says that God *"keeps His covenant and His lovingkindness to a thousandth generation with those who love Him and keep His commandments."* This means also that God will bless your children and your children's children because of *your* faithfulness.

When you are an obedient child, your Father will bring into your life a husband or a wife who is exceedingly and abundantly beyond anything you could ask or think. He will help you get that great job that you know you are not qualified for, and then give you the wisdom and grace to excel at it. As a faithful child, you will know that no matter what you are going through today, you will come out on top in the end. You will live each day with the confidence that no weapon formed against you will prosper.

Claim Your Inheritance

Sons have rights because they are family members and heirs. Slaves do not. Before you gave your life to the Lord, you were a slave. You were a slave to your temper, to your lusts and desires, or to bitterness and unforgiveness. Now that you are a son, whether male or female, you are no longer a slave. Christ has set you free, God has adopted you into His family, and all the rights and privileges of sonship are now yours. Because you are a son, you don't have to prove your identity and you don't have to earn your inheritance. You are already in your Father's will and He will never disinherit you. Stop thinking and acting like a slave. Don't live beneath your privileges.

Get the Attitude of an Heir

Remember that attitude determines altitude. Your attitude will make you or break you. It will determine whether you rise to your potential and claim your rightful inheritance as a son, or stay in the pigpen as a hired hand eating scraps. Until you *believe* you are a son, you will not *think* like a son or *act* like a son. You will keep reverting to past habits, behaviors, and thought patterns—the very things that keep you in a cycle of failure.

You have to get an attitude that reflects who you really are: "Wait a minute! My Daddy owns the cattle on a thousand hills. My Daddy owns all the silver and all the gold. My Daddy rules a great big kingdom, and because it belongs to Him, it also belongs to me!" Because of His love and generosity, the Father has included all His children equally in His will. A true son knows that whatever the Father has is his also. My sons know that if they need something, their Daddy will give it to them. As a child of God, you ought to know that your heavenly Daddy will see that you get everything you need.

Luke tells the story of the prodigal son, who asked his father for his inheritance early. Taking it, he left home and went into a far country, where he quickly wasted it. Broke, busted, and disgusted, he ended up feeding pigs for a living. In the middle of the pigpen, he had an attitude adjustment. "Wait a minute! I've had it with this pig slop! I'm going back home to my Daddy's house. Even his servants are better off than I am."

He came crawling back home, feeling unworthy to be anything more than a servant in his father's house. His father, who had been watching for him, saw him from a long way off. Running to his son, the father opened his arms and received him warmly and joyfully. The son did not deserve his father's love, but he received it because he was his father's son. This is a picture of our heavenly Father. Even though we don't deserve His blessing, His love, or His inheritance, our Daddy says, "I've got My arms open for you. I love you. Come on back to Me."

When the prodigal son returned, his father put a robe on his back, a ring on his finger, and shoes on his feet. These were symbols of his position as a *son*, not a servant. It was his father's way of saying, "You may have walked away from me, but I never stopped loving you and forgiving you. You are my son, and now you have come home again. Come on, let's party!" That's how God looks at us today. He gladly receives us as sons, not because we are good or because we deserve it, but because we say, "Daddy, I love You, and I need You in my life."

Do you know who you are in Christ? Do you know that you are a son of inheritance? Do you know that whatever belongs to Jesus belongs to you as a joint heir? When you do, you will stop letting fear control your life. You will stop begging God and start exercising your faith and boldly claiming your rightful inheritance. You will let go of the past. You will quit holding grudges against people who have hurt you. You will have peace and a calm assurance that no matter where you are right now, someday you will walk into your destiny.

You are a child of God and have the right to walk in His blessings, as long as you are walking in obedience to His Word and His will. God has a great inheritance for you, and it is time to claim it. The Lord says, "Get up, go in, and possess the land! It's yours. I have given it to you."

Maybe folks have beaten you down all your life and told you you're no good and will never amount to anything. Don't fall for that anymore. You are a son, part of a royal family, and it is time to claim your inheritance. Stop apologizing for God's blessings in your life. You are *supposed* to be blessed; you are a son of inheritance.

Claim Your Inheritance

God is saying, "I have placed the land before you, but you must go in and possess it. Don't despise your inheritance. It's there waiting for you. I left it for you in the will."

Adam and Eve lost their inheritance in the garden when the serpent tricked them. Jesus came to restore it. He has given you the authority to claim your inheritance, but you have to press toward the prize if you expect to win. It won't happen all at once; the Israelites did not conquer Canaan in a day. Even if you do not have it all together right now, *press toward the prize*. Your finances may be in bad shape, but *press toward the prize*. You may have a lot of family problems, but *press toward the prize*. At all times and in all things, follow Paul's example and *"press on toward the goal for the prize of the upward call of God in Christ Jesus"* (Philippians 3:14). It's your inheritance; reach out and claim it!

Maybe you are saying, "That's all well and good, but it's not working for me. I am trying to follow the Lord. I want to claim my inheritance, but I am still not seeing God's blessings in my life. Something is still holding me back. No matter what I do, I can't seem to get ahead." The problem may lie deep inside you with an issue that can stop you dead in your tracks and sabotage every positive thing you try to do. That issue has to do with *forgiveness*.

DON'T JUDGE MY FUTURE BY MY PAST

Chapter Fifteen

DROP THE CHARGES

Forgiveness is one of the principal themes of Scripture. In fact, the entire Gospel message centers on forgiveness, healing, and restoration. One of the biggest reasons for strife, turmoil, and difficulty in our lives and relationships is because we do not take this matter of forgiveness seriously enough. There is no telling how many problems we would solve or how many difficult situations we would resolve if we would only learn how to forgive and receive forgiveness.

Forgiveness goes against our grain as humans. It is human nature to hold a grudge or get an "attitude" when someone wounds or offends us. Our natural tendency is to press charges against those who hurt us. What is the cost of unforgiveness? Just look around at all the broken relationships, the shattered lives, and the hostility that exists between individuals, people groups, and nations because of our "natural" unwillingness to forgive.

God has shown us a different way. His nature is to forgive us in spite of what we do. This does not mean that God ignores or overlooks our sin. God's judgment of our sin cost Jesus His life. Jesus died for our sins so that we could be forgiven. As we grow in Christ as born-again believers, we too must learn to forgive others just as Christ has forgiven us. One of the clearest marks of spiritual maturity is our ability to forgive those who have hurt us and to let go of any bitterness they may have caused.

Jesus Himself set the example for us to follow. Many were the times when people came to Him and He comforted them with the words, "Your sins are forgiven." Even as He hung on the cross, He reached out in love toward those who hated Him, praying, *"Father forgive them; for they do not know what they are doing"* (Luke 23:34).

Throughout His earthly ministry, Jesus stressed the importance of forgiveness. Everything hinges on it: answers to our prayers, the health of our relationships, even our very spiritual welfare.

> *Therefore I say to you, all things for which you pray and ask, believe that you have received them, and they will be granted you. And whenever you stand praying, forgive, if you have anything against anyone, so that your Father who is in heaven may forgive you your transgressions. But if you do not forgive, neither will your Father who is in heaven forgive your transgressions* (Mark 11:24–26).

Jesus said we can have everything if we pray and use our faith, but we must forgive others or our prayers will not work. God's forgiveness of us is linked to our willingness to forgive others. If we expect God to act on our behalf, we must forgive.

Forgiveness Is a Decision

This illustrates a fundamental principle by which God operates: Whatever we give out is what will come back to us. Jesus said:

> *Be merciful, just as your Father is merciful. And do not pass judgment and you will not be judged; and do not condemn, and you shall not be condemned; pardon, and you will be pardoned. Give, and it will be given to you; good measure, pressed down, shaken together, running over, they will pour into your lap. For whatever measure you deal out to others, it will be dealt to you in return* (Luke 6:36–38).

Drop the Charges

We need to be givers, for what we give will be given back to us. If we give mercy, we will receive mercy; if we judge, we will be judged. If we forgive a little, we will be forgiven a little; if we forgive a lot, we will be forgiven a lot. How much forgiveness we receive depends on how much forgiveness we are willing to give. God will use the same standard with us that we use with others.

> *"God takes the forgiveness business very seriously."*

This tells us two things. First, God takes the forgiveness business very seriously, and so should we. Forgiveness is one of the key principles of the Christian life because it is a prerequisite for just about everything else. God gives us principles by which to live rather than formulas to follow. A principle is a fundamental truth that, when exercised, yields the same result every time. Every time we forgive, we open the door for God's blessings to flow. We untie His hands so He can begin to work on our behalf.

The second lesson is perhaps even more important because so many of us misunderstand on this point: *Forgiveness is not a feeling, but a decision.* The Lord has *commanded* us to forgive, and through the Holy Spirit He has given us the ability to do so. Before we came to Christ, we could never really consider such forgiveness; it was beyond our capacity. As new creatures in Christ, however, we can now do what we could not do before.

Forgiving those who have hurt us is not a matter of feelings, but a matter of faith and obedience. We forgive not because we feel like it or because we want to, but because we *choose* to do so in obedience to our Lord. When we *do* forgive, we show evidence that we are indeed new creatures because forgiveness is a natural character trait of God and His children.

Jesus *chose* to forgive from the cross. God *chose* to forgive us rather than hold our sins against us. I once heard about a young boy who was shot and killed by a neighbor for throwing a rock through a window. The boy's parents *chose* to walk in forgiveness toward the neighbor. There have been many other instances where people have lost children or other loved ones due to the carelessness or malice of someone else, yet have chosen to forgive and try to bring healing and restoration.

We need to be very careful any time we are tempted to say, "I *cannot* forgive…" because that is a lie. The truth is, we *will* not forgive. As long as we take that attitude, we endanger our relationship with the Lord and sabotage our future. Whether we like it or not, forgiveness is a choice, and we are responsible before God for how we choose.

God's nature is to forgive people who do not deserve to be forgiven. Through His Spirit, He has placed that same nature in all of us who are born again. He commands and expects us to walk in forgiveness whether we want to or not. Our sin nature is selfish, controlling, critical, and unforgiving. In Christ, though, we have a new nature that enables us to forgive undeserving people.

Come to think of it, there *are* no deserving people. None of us *deserve* God's forgiveness. God is under no obligation to forgive anyone. He forgave us because He chose to in accordance with His nature. That is all the more reason for us to forgive. Of all people, we who have experienced God's forgiveness for ourselves should be the most forgiving of others.

When we choose not to forgive, we choose to cut ourselves off from God's blessings and from His guiding, protecting hand on our lives. Our unwillingness to forgive puts us in big trouble with God. No mountains will move in our lives, no breakthroughs will come, and no miracles will occur. As long as we refuse to forgive, we will live under a spirit of failure.

Forgiveness is a choice, and how we choose will make the difference between success or failure, blessings or curses, and life or death.

Get Rid of the Baggage

Unforgiving people are usually guilt-ridden people. Because they have not forgiven those who have hurt them, they are unable to forgive themselves for their own mistakes. Consequently, they walk around under a constant burden of guilt.

Does that describe you? Is your life full of turmoil? Do you wrestle constantly with a feeling of guilt? You may have a forgiveness issue. A spirit of unforgiveness will rob you of the ability to be at peace with yourself. What you give out is what you get back. The same standard you use on others is the one God will use on you.

No matter how much you may pray for God's forgiveness, you will never find release until you are willing in your heart to release others from the things they have done to you. You have to reach the point in your spiritual walk where you can look at a person who hurt you and say, "I forgive you for what you did. I release you of all your debts, and I let it go." It is only when you completely release and forgive others for their sins against you that you can be totally released and forgiven for yours.

> *"Unforgiveness is nothing more than excess baggage that weighs you down."*

Unforgiveness is nothing more than excess baggage that weighs you down. It ties you mentally and emotionally to the very people you refuse to forgive, so that you drag them around with you wherever you go. Why should you give *anyone* that much power over you? Your release will come when you release them. The only people who can truly hurt you are the people you refuse to forgive. Even then, you are only hurting yourself *because* of them.

An unforgiving spirit causes us to build walls around ourselves. Every time we nurse a hurt or refuse to let go of an injury, we add one more brick to our wall. Eventually, we end up confined in a prison of our own making. Refusing to forgive those who hurt us is a way of trying to hold them hostage in our hearts. In reality, it is *we* who are the hostages—prisoners of our own bitterness.

Nothing is more difficult or unhealthy than living behind the walls of unforgiveness. It will cause you to lose sleep and to become hateful. It will eat away at your insides. Unforgiveness pumps highly toxic poison into your body, even breaking down your immune system so that you get sick more easily. It clouds your judgment and your perception so that you see all of life through a fog of bitterness and resentment. An unforgiving spirit saps your energy, your creativity, your initiative, your joy, and your vision. It traps you in a continuing cycle of failure and frustration.

Sometimes it is hard to tell if the problems we are facing are due to a forgiveness issue. Our tendency is to blame our troubles on anything or anybody other than ourselves. Consequently, we may be unable or unwilling to see that the source of the problem is internal.

Here is a simple test. If you suspect you may have a problem with forgiveness, ask yourself the following four questions. They will help you determine whether or not forgiveness is an issue in your life.

Have I been hurt by someone?

Do I keep thinking about what this person did?

Am I avoiding this person?

Do strong feelings of anger arise whenever I think about or happen to see this person?

If you answered "yes" to two or more of these questions, it is very likely that there is someone you need to forgive.

You cannot afford to allow resentment or an unforgiving spirit to destroy your life; you have too much to live for! Excess baggage is a liability. Assets minus liabilities equal net worth. What is your net worth? Are you bankrupt or blessed? If you have more baggage than assets, you have a negative net worth, which means you lack the resources to change your situation.

Why should your life be on hold simply because you won't forgive someone? Why squander your future over something that happened in the past? Get rid of your baggage of unforgiveness. If you are holding people hostage because of an injury they inflicted on you, release them and let it go. It is time to drop the charges.

Grant a Pardon

Few things in life are more disheartening than living under the cloud of someone else's unforgiveness. When you forgive someone who hurt you, you grant a double pardon—you pardon that person as well as yourself. Your forgiveness sets him free, and it also liberates your spirit. It opens the door for the power, grace, and love of God to begin to flow in your life once more. By learning to forgive, you learn to put away childish behavior and move into spiritual maturity.

Forgiving someone else for his offense lifts a great weight off of our shoulders. Our natural tendency when wronged is to seek revenge or try to punish those responsible. Sometimes we are reluctant to forgive because we think that in doing so, we are letting them off the hook. In reality, forgiveness lets *us* off the hook of God's judgment and makes it possible for Him to do things in us He has never been able to do before. As for the other people, once we truly forgive them, our desire for revenge or punishment will go away. If recompense is needed, we can leave it in the Lord's hands because the right of vengeance is His alone, and He will exercise it if necessary.

If you have any remaining doubt about the importance God places on our willingness to forgive, listen to these words from Jesus: *"If therefore you are presenting your offering at the altar, and there remember that your brother has something against you, leave your offering there before the altar, and go your way; first be reconciled to your brother, and then come and present your offering"* (Matthew 5:23–24). As far as God is concerned, taking care of a forgiveness issue is more important than worship or tithing or any other spiritual service or activity. Why? Because we cannot worship God in spirit and in truth or serve Him with honesty if we harbor unforgiveness in our hearts. To try to do so makes us hypocrites.

God says, "I don't want your money as long as you have bitterness in your heart." Even if *you* have no bitterness but know someone else does, you must go to that person. Once the Spirit of God makes you aware of the problem, it is your responsibility to take the initiative, even if you are not at fault and even if the other person does not make the first move. God wants you to forgive and release people who don't deserve it. After all, He forgave you, and you didn't deserve it. At the same time, remember that you cannot heal every situation because not everybody will let you. You are responsible to do your part, then you must leave the rest in the Lord's hands.

Forgiveness is absolutely essential to our personal holiness. The Lord has told us, *"You shall be holy for I am holy"* (Leviticus 11:45). Holiness has nothing to do with dressing a certain way or wearing our hair a certain way or saying all the right words at church or carrying a big Bible everywhere we go. God is not interested in external appearances; He looks into our hearts. Holiness comes from within and is all about lifestyle. It is about living and obeying the Word of God. Holiness is about the way we treat people.

Love is an aspect of holiness. The Bible says that God is love and that He loves all people. As His children, we too should be filled with love. How can we harbor hate toward someone and call ourselves born again? How can we hold resentment against a fellow Christian and still claim to love God? If we do, the Bible says we are lying.

> *If someone says, "I love God," and hates his brother, he is a liar; for the one who does not love his brother whom he has seen, cannot love God whom he has not seen. And this commandment we have from Him, that the one who loves God should love his brother also* (1 John 4:20–21).

No matter what we say we believe, as long as we harbor hatred, anger, or resentment in our hearts and refuse to forgive, we have no right to call ourselves Christians.

Jesus said that we are to love our enemies and pray for those who persecute us (see Matthew 5:44). This goes against our human instinct, which is what makes it so hard to do. Besides, the devil will do everything he can to keep us locked up in our bitterness and unforgiveness because he does not want us to be delivered. All that that unforgiveness will do is cause our wounds to fester. Once we let go of our hurt and bitterness and begin to pray for our enemies, God begins to change *us*. He cleanses our wounds with the blood of Jesus and binds them with His tender mercy. He releases us from the bonds of bitterness that have tied us to the injury, and although the memory of the hurt may remain, the pain will be gone.

Never pay back evil for evil. Remember that whatever you give is what you will get. The same standard you use toward others is the one God will use for you. Think about it. Do you *really* want God to treat *you* the way you treat others? Stop holding people hostage to their past offenses against you. It is time to grant them a pardon. Drop the charges.

Seventy Times Seven

Our forgiveness of others is a spiritual account that should never become overdrawn. We should never run out of our capacity or willingness to forgive. The degree to which we forgive others determines the degree to which God forgives us. Jesus illustrated the importance of this truth in a passage found in Matthew chapter 18.

> *"Truly I say to you, whatever you bind on earth shall have been bound in heaven; and whatever you loose on earth shall have been loosed in heaven. Again I say to you, that if two of you agree on earth about anything that they may ask, it shall be done for them by My Father who is in heaven. For where two or three have gathered together in My name, there am I in their midst." Then Peter came and said to Him, "Lord, how often shall my brother sin against me and I forgive him? Up to seven times?" Jesus said to him, "I do not say to you, up to seven times, but up to seventy times seven"* (Matthew 18:18–22).

Many believers have been taught that verse 18 refers to the binding and loosing of demons, but that interpretation goes against the context of the entire passage. Immediately prior to verse 18, Jesus was talking about restoring a brother who has sinned, and immediately after, He spoke on the scope of forgiveness. Jesus' words on binding and loosing, then, occur in the context of forgiveness.

One way to look at it is that whenever we bind someone on earth by refusing to forgive them, God binds us in heaven by shutting off the flow of blessing and joy and fellowship. When we loose someone by releasing them in forgiveness, God releases us.

After this, Peter asked Jesus how often he should forgive a brother who sinned against him. Since Jewish law required forgiveness of a person up to three times a day, Peter undoubtedly felt quite generous in offering to forgive seven times. Imagine his shock when Jesus told him to forgive seventy times seven!

153

Jesus' point is that there should be no limit to our forgiveness, either in our willingness or in its frequency. How often should we forgive? Very simply, as often as necessary. That's a tall order, impossible to fill in our own strength, which is why we need the power of the Holy Spirit working in our lives.

> *"How often should we forgive? Very simply, as often as necessary."*

This issue of forgiveness is so important that Jesus emphasized it with a sobering parable that illustrates the deadly peril we place ourselves in if we harbor an unforgiving spirit. In the story, a king called to account one of his slaves who owed him 10,000 talents. In today's economy that would be the equivalent of millions of dollars. When the slave was unable to pay, the king ordered him sold along with his family in repayment of the debt. The slave fell to the ground and begged for mercy, pledging to pay in full if given more time. Moved with compassion, the king forgave his slave of the entire debt.

The newly forgiven slave went out and promptly accosted a fellow slave who owed him a few dollars, demanding that he pay up. When the second slave begged for more time, the first slave refused to listen and had him thrown into debtor's prison. Word of this got back to the king, who called the first slave before him once again and said, *"You wicked slave, I forgave you all that debt because you entreated me. Should you not also have had mercy on your fellow-slave, even as I had mercy on you?"* (Matthew 18:32–33) The king then handed the slave over to the torturers until he paid his debt.

Jesus closed the story with the words, *"So shall My heavenly Father also do the same to you, if each of you does not forgive his brother from your heart"* (Matthew 18:35). Make no mistake about it, if we dance around this issue of forgiveness, we risk stepping right off the edge of the precipice. Our spiritual welfare is at stake. Let's not be number-crunchers when it comes to forgiveness. Let's not keep score or run up a tally sheet. It's simply not worth it. We need God's power and presence in our lives too much to block it out with an unforgiving spirit. No matter who it is, what they've done, or how often they do it, let's drop the charges.

Living the Love Walk

In Romans 8:29 Paul said that God has predestined all believers to be *"conformed to the image of His Son."* This means that we are supposed to be like Jesus in temperament, behavior, and spirit. One of the great distinguishing characteristics of being like Jesus is to have a heart of forgiveness. Such a heart must be carefully cultivated, and this takes time. Healthy cultivation requires good soil, fertile ground that promises a rich harvest.

Jesus told the story of a farmer who sowed his seed on four types of ground: hard-packed, rocky, thorny, and good. The seed on the first three kinds of soil did not prosper because they were "bad" ground. The seed on the "good" ground, however, produced a bumper crop.

In your response to the Lord, you are either good ground or bad ground. If you are good ground, you will grow and prosper, be fruitful, and experience victory. If, on the other hand, you are bad ground, you will block your own breakthrough because the seeds of God's Spirit will find no root.

Bad soil can be poisonous to plants by being either too acidic or too alkali. What are some of the "poisons" that may infect you, causing you to be bad ground? Here are some symptoms to look for: anger, bitterness, resentment, hatred, guilt, pride, unforgiveness, inability to pray or to understand the Word of God—the list could go on. When you are not good ground, everything in your life will be turned upside down. If your heart is not right, nothing else will be right. You can receive only a little from the Lord but cannot be filled up because you are not good ground.

Characteristics of good ground include humility and a forgiving spirit, as well as *"love, joy, peace, patience, kindness, goodness, faithfulness, gentleness, self-control"* (Galatians 5:22–23), and many others. The more these qualities manifest in your life, the more like Jesus you are becoming. Forgiveness is the key. An unforgiving spirit will dam up the river and stop the flow of the Spirit's work in your life.

Essentially, being good ground means imitating God. Paul issued this challenge to the Ephesians: *"Therefore be imitators of God, as beloved children; and walk in love, just as Christ also loved you, and gave Himself up for us, an offering and a sacrifice to God as a fragrant aroma"* (Ephesians 5:1–2). God has called all of us who know Him to a "love walk."

The "love walk" is the walk of faith, not of sight. When we walk in love we walk not by feelings but in obedience to the Word of God. This involves forgiving people who do not deserve forgiveness—people we don't *want* to forgive. Remember that forgiveness is a choice. It is a walk of maturity in which we choose to lay aside our own feelings and do what God wants. To walk in love means casting off the baggage of anger, resentment, bitterness, and unforgiveness that have bound us to the hurts and offenses of the past. Walking in love means dropping the charges.

Do you need to forgive someone? Release that person and let him go. Cut the bonds of resentment and bitterness that have tied you to the people who hurt you. Don't give them that much control over your life. God is saying, "If you want My help, drop the charges. If you want My healing, drop the charges. If you want to be in My will, drop the charges."

There are some things you will never figure out. That's why you have to walk by faith and not by sight. That's why you have to give all your anger, bitterness, and resentment to God and walk away. You can't afford to press charges because you need all of God's help that you can get. Dropping the charges and forgiving those who hurt you will help you get your past behind you once and for all.

Folks may lie about you. Oh well; drop the charges. They may take advantage of you. Even so, drop the charges. They may attack you; still, drop the charges. It doesn't matter who said what, who did what, or who started it; drop the charges.

When you drop the charges, the gates of heaven will open wide and God's blessings will flow in your life and to others through you. When you drop the charges, your prayers will be answered. Your life will turn around, your failures will change to successes, and your defeats will become victories. It may not happen overnight, but it will happen. You will know the joy and peace of the Lord, and a bright and beautiful future will open up before you. All you have to do is walk the love walk. All you have to do is drop the charges.

Chapter Sixteen

THE ARROWS OF DELIVERANCE

It was a grim time for the nation of Israel. King Ahab, who had little regard for the faith of his fathers, had married Jezebel, daughter of the king of the Sidonians and, like her people, a dedicated worshiper of the false god Baal. It didn't take long for Ahab to join his queen in her pagan worship.

Ahab's marriage to Jezebel caused great trouble for the children of God. Jezebel hated the God of Israel and did everything she could to lead His people astray. She personally supported and protected hundreds of priests of Baal and was directly instrumental in the slaughter of many prophets and servants of the Lord. Her forceful personality overwhelmed even her husband, the king. As wicked as he was in regard to intrigue, cunning, and sheer evil, Ahab was no match for his wife. Under Jezebel's terrifying influence, the vast majority of the people of Israel succumbed to Baal worship.

At such a time as this, God needed a powerful voice in the land, so He raised up Elijah as His prophet and spokesman. Elijah was a man of great anointing who possessed a deep and abiding love for both God and his nation. Through Elijah, God confronted the

157

wickedness and idolatry of Ahab, Jezebel, and the people, even withholding rain in the land for three and a half years. Elijah served the Lord faithfully and performed numerous miracles, including calling down the fire of God on Mount Carmel to consume a sacrifice and prove that Baal was no god at all. King Ahab died during Elijah's lifetime, but Jezebel remained.

In due time the Lord raised up a man named Elisha to succeed Elijah. After serving faithfully for many years as Elijah's aide and servant, Elisha asked for and received from God a double portion of the anointing that had been on Elijah. During his prophetic ministry, Elisha also performed many miraculous signs. It was during Elisha's life that Jezebel was put to death in fulfillment of God's judgment prophesied years earlier.

Ahab and Jezebel were gone, but the damage was done. The nation of Israel was steeped in Baal worship and under constant threat of invasion from surrounding nations. Shortly before Elisha died, the king of Israel sought him out for help and counsel in the face of the latest threat.

When Elisha became sick with the illness of which he was to die, Joash the king of Israel came down to him and wept over him and said, "My father, my father, the chariots of Israel and its horsemen!" And Elisha said to him, "Take a bow and arrows." So he took a bow and arrows. Then he said to the king of Israel, "Put your hand on the bow." And he put his hand on it, then Elisha laid his hands on the king's hands. And he said, "Open the window toward the east," and he opened it. Then Elisha said, "Shoot!" And he shot. And he said, "The Lord's arrow of victory, even the arrow of victory over Syria; for you shall defeat the Syrians at Aphek until you have destroyed them." Then he said, "Take the arrows," and he took them. And he said to the king of Israel, "Strike the ground," and he struck it three times and stopped. So the man of God was angry with him and said, "You should have struck five or six times, then you would have struck Syria until you would have destroyed it. But now you shall strike Syria only three times" (2 Kings 13:14–19).

The Arrows of Deliverance

This story illustrates the relationship between faith and deliverance. Israel was sorely pressed by the Syrians, and Joash, the king of Israel, came to Elisha to find out what to do. Elisha instructed him to shoot an arrow in the direction of the enemy. This was symbolic of the promise that the Lord would give Israel victory.

Next, Elisha told the king to take his remaining arrows and strike the ground with them. Joash struck the ground three times, then stopped. The context of the passage suggests that the king lacked enthusiasm for this exercise, which is why he did not perform it more vigorously. It may be that in his heart he doubted the Lord or Elisha. Perhaps this was not the kind of "help" he expected. He may have hoped to get specific instructions on how to fight the enemy, or tips on strategy. Instead, he was told to shoot one arrow, then strike the ground with the others.

At any rate, Elisha was angry with the king over his lackadaisical response. Because Joash struck the ground only three times, Israel would defeat their enemy only three times. Had the king struck the ground more enthusiastically, God would have given him complete and total victory.

Elisha was disappointed with the king's lack of enthusiasm. He had hoped that Joash would get excited over the fact that God was about to deliver Israel from the hand of the enemy. The king's arrows represented deliverance. But because he expected little deliverance, he got little deliverance.

God has given each of us a quiver full of arrows of deliverance. In order for them to work, we must set them to the bow and shoot them with faith and enthusiasm, confident that the Lord will bring about our deliverance from everything that holds us back.

The Arrow of Worship

One of the arrows of deliverance in our quiver is the arrow of worship. Enthusiastic, passionate worship honors the Lord and activates the work of the Spirit on our behalf. John 4:23 says that the Father seeks worshipers who will worship Him in spirit and truth. How often have you seen people in church who never get into the spirit of worship and praise? How often have you been guilty of the same thing? The preacher does his best to stir us to excitement about the things of God, while we just stand around with our hands in our pockets. He tries to inspire us to shout in victory, but we remain silent, tight-lipped in defiance.

If we want to see the Lord work mightily in our midst, we have to get excited about our faith. Otherwise, very little will happen. Psalm 47:1 says, *"O clap your hands, all peoples; shout to God with the voice of joy."* One thing that the Bible makes very clear is that God is looking for enthusiastic worshipers.

> *"Enthusiastic, passionate worship honors the Lord and activates the work of the Spirit on our behalf."*

When you need a major victory, give the Lord major worship. Too much is at stake to allow the enthusiasm of your worship to flag. King Joash had enough faith for only a few victories. Had he been enthusiastic enough to tap his arrows on the ground five or six times, he would have experienced total victory. Because he went only part way, he achieved only partial success. God stops when you stop.

Our natural tendency when faced with trouble is to worry rather than worship. Often, when hard times come, the first thing we do is drop out of church. We separate ourselves from the ministry of the Word and prayer and the fellowship and encouragement of the body of Christ just when we need them the most. Whatever you do, don't drop out. You will never become an overcomer as long as you remain passive about your walk with the Lord or drop out at the first sign of pressure.

Believers who overcome worship the Lord with passion and enthusiasm. Whether at church or away, they avail themselves of every opportunity to sing, shout, pray, praise, and study the Word of God. God is looking to bless enthusiastic people who will get excited about His promises and worship Him in spirit and truth. Do you want victory and deliverance in your life? Learn to shoot your arrows of worship consistently and enthusiastically.

The Arrow of Prayer

Prayer is another potent arrow of deliverance that is available to us at all times. Our supply of prayer arrows can never be exhausted. Paul encouraged us to *"pray without ceasing"* (1 Thessalonians 5:17), and *"Be anxious for nothing, but in everything by prayer and supplication with thanksgiving let your requests be made known to God"* (Philippians 4:6). Prayer is indispensable as a weapon of our warfare: *"With all prayer and petition pray at all times in the Spirit, and with this in view, be on the alert with all perseverance and petition for all the saints"* (Ephesians 6:18). James 5:16 assures us that *"the effective prayer of a righteous man can accomplish much."*

The British poet Alfred, Lord Tennyson wrote, "More things are wrought by prayer than this world dreams of." Prayer energizes the activity of the Holy Spirit in our daily lives and in the world as a whole. It connects us with the infinite resources of heaven and helps align our hearts and minds with the heart and mind of God.

King Hezekiah of Judah was sick, and the prophet Isaiah told him that he was going to die and needed to get his affairs in order. The king needed a miracle, so he turned his face to the wall and prayed (see 2 Kings 20:1–7). God had told Hezekiah to prepare for death, but when the king prayed for healing, the Lord heard his prayer and added fifteen years to his life. Hezekiah shot an arrow of prayer, and God brought him deliverance.

Sometimes when you need a miracle, you have to turn away from people and turn to the Lord. When your back is against the wall and the dogs of the enemy have you at bay, give yourself to prayer. If you are sick and can't get well, you need a specialist, someone who can look at your x-rays and say, "I know what to do. I know how to fix this problem. I know how to bring deliverance here." Do you need deliverance? Heed the words of the old gospel hymn:

"Have we trials and temptations? Is there trouble anywhere?
We should never be discouraged, take it to the Lord in prayer.

Can we find a friend so faithful who will all our sorrows share?
Jesus knows our every weakness, take it to the Lord in prayer."

The Arrow of the Word of God

The Word of God supplies us with countless arrows of deliverance for our quiver. Whatever the need, God provides for it in His Word. If you need healing, shoot the arrow of Matthew 8:17: "*[Jesus] Himself took our infirmities and carried away our diseases,*" or James 5:15: "*The prayer offered in faith will restore the one who is sick, and the Lord will raise him up.*"

If you are trying to start a business and are having a hard time getting it off the ground, launch the arrow of Isaiah 48:17: "*Thus says the LORD, your Redeemer, the Holy One of Israel, 'I am the LORD your God, who teaches you to profit, who leads you in the way you should go.' *" Whenever you sense the enemy pressing his attack on you or on your family, fight back with the arrow of Isaiah 54:17: " *'No weapon that is formed against you shall prosper; and every tongue that accuses you in judgment you will condemn. This is the heritage of the servants of the LORD, and their vindication is from Me,' declares the LORD.*"

When the pressures and anxieties of life seem overwhelming and you fear that you are about to go under, find deliverance in the arrow of Psalm 34:19: "*Many are the afflictions of the righteous, but the LORD delivers him out of them all,*" or Matthew 11:28: "*Come to Me, all who are weary and heavy-laden, and I will give you rest.*"

The great thing about the arrows of deliverance that God has given you is their variety. If for some reason one arrow does not do the job, you have other arrows that will. When hell or high water come against you, shoot the arrow of Isaiah 43:2: "*When you pass through the waters, I will be with you; and through the rivers, they will not overflow you. When you walk through the fire, you will not be scorched, nor will the flame burn you.*" When your finances are tight and you wonder where the rent, mortgage, grocery, or car payment money is going to come from, pull from your quiver Philippians 4:19: "*And my God shall supply all your needs according to His rich-*

es in glory in Christ Jesus," or Psalm 37:25: *"I have been young, and now I am old; yet I have not seen the righteous forsaken or his descendants begging bread."*

If you are faithfully serving the Lord, tithing, and trying to be obedient, yet things are still tough, launch the arrow of Deuteronomy 28:1–2: *"Now it shall be, if you diligently obey the LORD your God, being careful to do all His commandments which I command you today, the LORD your God will set you high above all the nations of the earth. And all these blessings shall come upon you and overtake you, if you will obey the LORD your God."*

When people try to hold your past against you and tell you that you are worthless, fire off the arrow of 2 Corinthians 5:17: *"Therefore if anyone is in Christ, he is a new creature; the old things passed away; behold, new things have come,"* or Romans 8:16–17: *"The Spirit Himself bears witness with our spirit that we are children of God, and if children, heirs also, heirs of God and fellow-heirs with Christ, if indeed we suffer with Him so that we may also be glorified with Him."*

Anytime Jesus faced difficult situations, He reached down in His bag of arrows and pulled out the Word. That was how He overcame Satan during His forty-day period of temptation in the wilderness. The devil was no match for the arrows of God's Word that Jesus released.

God's Word will stand forever. Jesus said, *"Heaven and earth will pass away, but My words shall not pass away"* (Matthew 24:35). We can trust the Word of God because it is true and living, not the dead words of dead men. Hebrews 4:12 says, *"For the word of God is living and active and sharper than any two-edged sword, and piercing as far as the division of soul and spirit, of both joints and marrow, and able to judge the thoughts and intentions of the heart."* His Word is a lamp to our feet and a light to our path (see Psalm 119:105). The Word of God brings deliverance.

The Arrow of the Blood of Jesus

With the arrows of worship, prayer, and the Word of God, we have a powerful arsenal for waging spiritual warfare, against which the devil cannot stand. Satan will not give up without a fight, though. He will constantly try to undermine our faith in God and our confidence in the

163

> "Whatever the devil thought he had on us was canceled when Jesus died and rose again."

spiritual weapons at our disposal. There is one weapon, however, that the devil can do absolutely nothing about: the blood of Jesus.

Our spiritual enemy has a plan to hold us in bondage, but Jesus died to bring us deliverance. All the works of the devil—all his plans and plots and schemes—were destroyed by the blood of Jesus. Whatever went before, whatever we may have done as slaves of sin, whatever contract the devil thought he had on us was canceled when Jesus died and rose again.

Satan's defeat is dramatically described in the twelfth chapter of Revelation:

And I heard a loud voice in heaven, saying, "Now the salvation, and the power, and the kingdom of our God and the authority of His Christ have come, for the accuser of our brethren has been thrown down, who accuses them before our God day and night. And they overcame him because of the blood of the Lamb and because of the word of their testimony, and they did not love their life even to death" (Revelation 12:10–11).

The blood of Jesus and the word of our testimony to His saving power together form a kind of "one-two punch" that Satan, our accuser, cannot not ignore, deny, or counteract. He has to either flee or end up lying on the canvas. Our brethren in the early church overcame the devil by the blood of Jesus and by the word of their testimony, and we can too. *"Jesus Christ is the same yesterday and today, yes and forever"* (Hebrews 13:8). He never changes, so that which delivered believers two thousand years ago will deliver us today.

If there is one arrow that the devil hates the most, it is the arrow of the blood of Jesus. The Lord has turned the tables on the devil. Jesus' blood broke Satan's power over us, destroyed the power of death, and set us free. Through the blood of Jesus we can now exercise authority over the powers of darkness.

No matter what kind of bondage you may be in, the blood of Jesus can set you free. I don't care if it is an addiction to lust, sex, food, drugs, cigarettes, or alcohol that drives you, the blood of Jesus can deliver you. When nothing else could help, the blood of Jesus set me free. When no treatment center had any answers, when no counselor could bring me lasting help, the arrow of the blood of Jesus slew the dragon and rescued me. What the blood of Jesus did for me, it can do for anyone.

The Arrow of Perseverance

One of the toughest battles we will ever fight in our Christian life is the battle against discouragement. Satan loves to fill our minds with thoughts that tell us how hopeless our struggle is. That is why the Lord has included in our quiver of deliverance weapons the arrow of perseverance.

Even when you are faithful to worship, pray, speak the Word of God into your situation, and plead the blood of Jesus, change will not always come right away. That is when you must launch your arrow of perseverance and simply hang tough. God will deliver you in His time and in His way, and He will not be late. Paul said to not *"lose heart in doing good, for in due time we shall reap if we do not grow weary"* (Galatians 6:9). In other words, hang in there, because your deliverance is on its way!

In the Old Testament, Moses was a "type" of Christ while Pharaoh was a "type" of the devil. Moses did not simply suggest or request to Pharaoh to let Israel go; he *demanded* that Pharaoh let them go. Eventually Pharaoh did so, but not before a long struggle with Moses in a head-to-head battle of the wills and a contest between the God of Israel and the so-called gods of Egypt. Israel's freedom was certain to come, but they and Moses had to persevere until the day of their deliverance arrived. In the meantime, their situation got worse before it got better.

Many times that is the way it is with us as well. We may not always understand why God does not deliver us right away, but we need to release our arrow of perseverance, hold on to our faith, and trust that God is working our situation out. He has His own reasons for delaying, and they are always for our good. If nothing else, tribulation toughens and matures us because it teaches us to trust and shows us that in Christ we can endure more than we ever dreamed possible.

Satan hates the bag of deliverance arrows that we carry because he knows that they can defeat and destroy him. That is why he is always trying to convince us not to use them. He floods our minds with doubts and questions about the truth and accuracy of the Bible. When we are trying to pray, he will fill our minds with all sorts of distracting thoughts so that prayer becomes a real struggle. He tries to stir up strife and division in our church so that our spirit and atmosphere for worship are destroyed.

If you are continually going through the same problems over and over again, it is because you are not shooting your arrows of deliverance. Perhaps one reason you have problems year after year is because you have lost your enthusiasm.

The next time trouble comes your way, pull the arrows of deliverance out of your quiver, set them to your bow, and release them in faith. The next time you feel like you simply can't go on, open your mouth and proclaim, "I am strong in the Lord. I can do all things through Christ who strengthens me." One thing you must never do is give up; that's just what the devil wants you to do. Instead, cast all your cares on the Lord, knowing that He cares for you. Shoot your arrows of deliverance with enthusiasm and confidence, and just watch what God does for you!

No matter how strong you think you are, you are not strong enough to defeat the devil without God's arrows of deliverance and the sword of the Spirit, which is His Word. Defeating the enemy calls for enthusiastic, confident faith on your part, as well as your active involvement in the fight. The kingdom of heaven suffers violence and the violent take it by force says Matthew 11:12. It is time to take the arrows out of your quiver and fight back in Jesus' name.

God has already provided for your deliverance. All He is waiting for is for you to use the arrows He has given you and fight the good fight of faith. He longs for you to be enthusiastic, to be passionate in your love for Him. God moves mountains for people who are passionate about their faith. He draws near to those who are determined to touch Him. God brings deliverance and victory to all who will press toward Him and not give up. To those who persevere, He also gives *joy*.

DON'T JUDGE MY FUTURE BY MY PAST

Chapter Seventeen

JOY LIKE A RIVER

What do health experts say is America's number one health problem today? Depression. Millions of Americans are miserable and have trouble coping with everyday life because they live in a chronic state of sadness. Why? One reason for this widespread depression is that so many people look for happiness in the wrong places. They look to sex, money, possessions, a fancy car, a fancy house, power, and influence to satisfy them. Some even look to other people to bring happiness and fulfillment into their lives.

Material possessions will never satisfy us. We will never find lasting happiness in the things of this world. Inside each of us is an emptiness, a void that surrounds the universal question, "What is the meaning of life?" That void cries to be filled, and we will try to fill it with anything we can. Our problem is that most of the time, the things we try don't work, and we end up just as hungry and just as unfulfilled as before.

There is no question that certain pleasures can bring happiness. Building our lives on the pursuit of happiness, however, is doomed to failure because happiness does not last. Happiness depends on our

> *"If God is the true focus of our lives, then our happiness is assured."*

environment, our external circumstances, and even on how we feel physically, and these things change all the time.

True and lasting happiness comes only when we build our lives on something that does not change—something that will fill that aching void inside us. The theme of the entire Old Testament Book of Ecclesiastes is the futility of seeking happiness in the things of the world. After looking unsuccessfully for happiness in knowledge, drink, sex, the pursuit of pleasure, and every other avenue that the mind and heart of man could conceive, the writer ends with these words: *"The conclusion, when all has been heard, is: fear God and keep His commandments, because this applies to every person. Because God will bring every act to judgment, everything which is hidden, whether it is good or evil"* (Ecclesiastes 12:13–14).

"Fear God and keep His commandments." That is the unchanging reality—the *only* reality in which we can find true happiness. If God is the true focus of our lives, then our happiness is assured. Psalm 37:4 says, *"Delight yourself in the LORD; and He will give you the desires of your heart."* This is a happiness that goes deeper than the happiness the world offers because it has God as its source. It is the kind of happiness that the Bible calls *joy.*

The Word of God links joy inseparably with our relationship with the Lord:

> *If you abide in Me, and My words abide in you, ask whatever you wish, and it shall be done for you. By this is My Father glorified, that you bear much fruit, and so prove to be My disciples. Just as the Father has loved Me, I have also loved you; abide in My love. If you keep My commandments, you will abide in My love; just as I have kept My Father's commandments, and abide in His love. These things I have spoken to you, that My joy may be in you, and that your joy may be*

made full. This is My commandment, that you love one another, just as I have loved you (John 15:7–12).

Do you want to know real joy? Learn to abide in Christ. Look to your relationship with Him to find the joy you crave. Happiness depends on your circumstances; joy does not. Joy is an outlook on life that comes from the Lord. If you have the Lord in your life, you can be full of joy even in the midst of difficult circumstances. When you taste joy, you drink from a well of endless supply. How much you drink and how often are up to you. Since the world did not give you joy, the world cannot take it away.

Sin Will Steal Your Joy

It is possible, however, to lose your joy. When things are not right between you and the Lord, your joy goes away. An incident in the life of King David provides a good illustration. David had been greatly blessed by the Lord, but somewhere along the line he began to feel as though the rules did not apply to him. One of the dangers of being richly blessed by God is that we can forget that the principles of God's Word are the same for everyone. If something is a sin for the servant, it is also a sin for the king. Sin will steal your joy.

One spring, at the time when kings normally led their troops into battle, David sent his army out under the command of his generals while he remained in Jerusalem. That was his first mistake. From his rooftop one evening, David saw a beautiful woman bathing, and he lusted after her in his heart. Her name was Bathsheba, and she was the wife of Uriah, one of David's most capable and loyal generals.

One thing quickly led to another. David brought Bathsheba into his palace and committed adultery with her. When he found out that she was pregnant with his child, he tried to cover up what had happened. He brought Uriah home on leave in the hopes that the man would sleep with his wife and take care of the problem. When that did not work, David became desperate—desperate enough to arrange for Uriah to be killed in battle so that David would then be free to take Bathsheba as his wife. If David had been out leading his troops instead of idling around at home, he never would have fallen into sin.

God sent a prophet named Nathan to confront David about his sins. The king responded with repentance and confession. David's sin had disrupted his fellowship with the Lord, and as a result, David lost the joy he had once known. Until his fellowship with God was restored, his joy could not be restored. David expressed his repentance in a psalm:

Be gracious to me, O God, according to Thy lovingkindness; according to the greatness of Thy compassion blot out my transgressions. Wash me thoroughly from my iniquity and cleanse me from my sin. For I know my transgressions, and my sin is ever before me. Against Thee, Thee only, I have sinned, and done what is evil in Thy sight, so that Thou art justified when Thou dost speak, and blameless when Thou dost judge....Create in me a clean heart, O God, and renew a steadfast spirit within me. Do not cast me away from Thy presence, and do not take Thy Holy Spirit from me. Restore to me the joy of Thy salvation, and sustain me with a willing spirit. Then I will teach transgressors Thy ways, and sinners will be converted to Thee (Psalm 51:1–4, 10–13).

David recognized that his joy was linked to his relationship with God, which is why he prayed, *"Restore to me the joy of Thy salvation."* He came clean about his sin, made no excuses, and did not try to shift the blame. David was honest with God, and God forgave him. Although David suffered physical consequences of his sin for the rest of his life, his fellowship with God was restored, and so was his joy. Psalm 32 is an expression of David's joy in this renewed relationship:

How blessed is he whose transgression is forgiven, whose sin is covered! How blessed is the man to whom the Lord does not impute iniquity, and in whose spirit there is no deceit! When I kept silent about my sin, my body wasted away through my groaning all day long. For day and night Thy hand was heavy upon me; my vitality was drained away as with the fever heat of summer. I acknowledged my sin to Thee, and my iniquity I did not hide; I said, "I will confess my transgressions to the Lord"; and Thou didst forgive the guilt of my sin. Therefore, let everyone who is godly pray to Thee in a time when Thou mayest be found; surely in a flood of great waters they will not reach him. Thou art my hiding place; Thou dost preserve me from trouble; Thou dost surround me with songs of deliverance (Psalm 32:1–7).

David fell into sin and lost all of his joy in the Lord. Let his experience be a warning. Take a firm stand against sin in your life, or you will fall into it as David did. If that happens, you will suffer not only broken fellowship with the Lord, but a loss of joy as well. Sin will steal your joy, but honest confession and repentance will restore it. The depth of your joy is directly related to the closeness of your walk with the Lord.

Joy Comes From Walking With the Lord

David's sin caused him to lose the joy of his salvation. As you walk with the Lord, a natural joy should bubble forth in your life—a general sense of well-being and favor that is not due to natural sources. If you know you are saved yet do not have joy, then there is probably something wrong in your relationship with Christ. A strong relationship with Him will fill you with the joy of heaven even if you are going through hell and high water on earth.

If your life lacks joy, take a close look inside yourself to see what is wrong. Are there sins you have not confessed? If so, bring them before God. You will never have joy until you deal with them. Do you have a "heart condition" that God needs to heal? David prayed, *"Create in me a clean heart, O God, and renew a steadfast spirit within me."* Perhaps that needs to be your prayer as well. Don't expect to be joyful in the Lord until you have dealt honestly and openly with any sin and disobedience in your life. Whatever the issue, as soon as you come clean and repent, joy will not be far behind: *"For His anger is but for a moment, His favor is for a lifetime; weeping may last for the night, but a shout of joy comes in the morning"* (Psalm 30:5).

Jesus said that those who keep His commandments and walk in love will be full of His joy. Joy comes from walking the "love walk" with the Lord. This joy has nothing to do with your material possessions or the outward circumstances of your life. It is a state of mind that enables you to smile even in the midst of great trouble or opposition. The joy of the Lord assures you that no matter what is going on right now, everything will be all right in the end.

A life with no joy is not much fun. Discouragement and depression will drain your energy and make you want to quit. Draw near to the Lord and He will draw near to you. When you walk close to Christ, His strength makes you stronger. As He fills you with His joy, His joy becomes your strength.

> *"A life with no joy is not much fun."*

Walking with the Lord strengthens your ability to trust Him. It helps you learn to be anxious for nothing, but pray over everything. Worry is the great enemy of joy. The two cannot coexist. Life is full of things you could worry about, but God said to pray instead and put everything in His hands. Simply release all your worries and burdens to the Lord, and He will replace them with peace and joy.

Joy is a fruit of the Spirit, which means it does not come through the flesh. As long as things are right between you and God, you will have joy. If you start walking according to the flesh, your joy will depart. It is a principle of spiritual life. Your joy is affected by how you live.

Joy cannot abide in the presence of bitterness or unforgiveness. It is impossible to be bitter and joyful at the same time. Likewise, joy and an unforgiving spirit are alien to each other. The Bible says that if you are not right with other people, you are not right with God, and unless you are right with God, you will not have joy in your life. Do you want joy in your life? Release those folks you have refused to forgive. Let go of your hurts and grudges. As long as you hold a grudge in your heart or wear a chip on your shoulder, you will have no room for joy.

Jesus said that if you abide in Him and His words abide in you that your joy will be made full. Joy arises from your relationship with the person of the Lord Jesus Christ. As long as you abide in Him and walk in the center of His will, His joy will fill your heart. Even if all your friends fail you, the joy of the Lord will never fail. People may walk out on you, but the joy of the Lord will never abandon you. Hard times may turn your life upside down, but the joy of the Lord will help keep you on an even keel. When life threatens to take you down, the joy of the Lord will help you overcome.

Joy Overcomes the World

In Philippians 4:4, the apostle Paul said, *"Rejoice in the Lord always; again I will say, rejoice!"* He knew all about the emotions we feel when we hook up with the Lord. Rejoicing is the overflow of the joy that bubbles up in our spirits when we know the Lord. We get so full of joy that we cannot contain it any longer, and it comes out with a shout or a song, a smile or a laugh or even, sometimes, a tear.

The presence of the Lord is a joyful place. Psalm 100 tells us to *"shout joyfully to the LORD, all the earth. Serve the LORD with gladness; come before Him with joyful singing...Enter His gates with thanksgiving, and His courts with praise. Give thanks to Him, bless His name"* (Psalm 100:1–2, 4). In other words, we are to put on a joyful heart and serve the Lord with a smile on our face and thanksgiving and praise on our lips.

> *"The presence of the Lord is a joyful place."*

With all the reasons we have to rejoice, it is hard to understand why so many Christians look like they were baptized in pickle juice. They always seem to have frowns on their faces and a sour attitude about life. Sometimes they go on and on about how hard it is to be a Christian. Make no mistake, the Christian life does have its challenges. In our walk with the Lord, we face many trials and tribulations, mainly because we live in a fallen world. At the same time, we have His promise that because He abides in us, we can overcome the world. Sometimes being a Christian may seem hard, but in the long run, *not* being a Christian is much harder.

What was your life like before you knew the Lord? How about the time you came within a hairsbreadth of killing yourself, or the struggle you had trying to kick drugs or alcohol? What about the abuse, or the pain of growing up in a broken home? What about the general hopelessness you felt about life? Compared to these, what's so hard about being a Christian? Jesus set you free from all that. If you are committed to following the Lord, *nothing* that happened before you knew Christ can prevent you from claiming the future that is yours in Him.

It is an established fact that happy, joyful people are generally healthier and live longer than people who are not. This lines up with the verse in Proverbs that says, *"A joyful heart is good medicine, but a broken spirit dries up the bones"* (Proverbs 17:22). In other words, when you are cheerful, it's good to be alive, but when you are depressed, life stinks.

Let's face it, hardships are a part of life. Times of depression will come when you feel trapped in a particular situation and can see no way out. Sometimes your mind can be your own worst enemy. That is why it is important to focus your mind on the Lord; for He has made a way for you to escape. You are not trapped, and in due time God will bring you out of your trouble. No matter how distressing they may seem, your difficulties are only temporary and will eventually pass away.

Storms last only for a season. Remember that although weeping may last for the night, joy comes in the morning. Even though the context of that verse is God's judgment, the principle is true for all the hardships you face. Whatever you may be going through now, God will at some point turn it around. As surely as spring follows winter and sunrise follows night, God will cause you to triumph in Christ Jesus.

Jesus said, *"In the world you have tribulation, but take courage; I have overcome the world"* (John 16:33). In other words, no trouble we face can destroy us because in Christ we will win before it's all over. The same Jesus who gives us joy also has overcome the world. His joy in us enables us to do the same. With His joy in our hearts, we can face the worst trials of our lives with confidence and assurance, knowing that those trials will eventually pass and we will emerge victorious on the other side.

Joy Comes From Praise

Praise is one of the surest and quickest ways to stir up joy in our spirits. Sometimes we praise the Lord because we are already happy, but at other times we do it because we are fighting for our faith. No matter who we are, heaviness of spirit descends on us from time to time. Praise is one way to dispel the heaviness and replace it with joy. Isaiah 61:3 speaks of the Lord coming to give His people *"the garment of praise for the spirit of heaviness"* (KJV). It is hard to be down or to stay down when we are lifting our eyes, our hands, and our voices in praise to our Lord.

Joy and praise go hand in hand. Sometimes our praise may be loud and boisterous, but we should never praise the Lord for the purpose of drawing attention to ourselves. True praise focuses our attention exclusively on God. Rather than drawing attention to ourselves, in genuine praise we tend to lose ourselves in Him. We praise the Lord because we need His strength and because we need His joy.

As Christians, we will never experience the fullness of true joy until we learn how to praise the Lord. There is something about true praise that causes joy to rise up in our souls. Somehow it invigorates us and infuses us with new strength and energy and spirit. Praise also has a powerful effect on our faith. The more we worship and praise God, the stronger our faith will become. For one thing, praise activates the free flow of the Spirit in our lives so that we can see more through the eyes of faith rather than through the eyes of flesh. For another, praise helps us adjust our attitude so that we see the circumstances of our lives in a different light.

When trouble comes your way, you can either blame God or you can praise your way to a new attitude. You can either throw in the towel or you can sing during your midnight hour. When Paul and Silas were in the Philippian jail, cold, damp, and bruised and sore from their beatings, at midnight they *"were praying and singing hymns of praise to God"* (Acts 16:25). All of a sudden the ground shook, the prison doors opened, and the prisoners' chains fell off. Praise brought divine deliverance. Not even the dismal environs of a prison could dampen their joy, and their praise brought it to full flower.

If you want to improve the atmosphere on your job or at home or wherever, try establishing a habit and a mind-set of praise. The more you praise, the more joy will flow in your heart. With the joy of the Lord as your strength, you can be confident that He has everything under control. Even if the devil roars in like a flood, God will raise up a standard against him. Joy will assure you that the Lord is bigger than all your problems and that He will turn everything around in your life.

The very first miracle that Jesus performed was turning water into wine, and He wants to do the same for you today. He wants to turn your ordinary life into a life filled with the wine of joy. He wants to turn your sadness into gladness and your mourning into dancing; to give you beauty for ashes, the oil of joy for mourning, and the garment of praise for the spirit of heaviness. If your cup is empty, He can fill it with fresh, new wine from a never-ending supply, the wine of a bubbling joy that the world can neither explain nor take away.

Joy will help you shake off the dust of the past, as well as the trouble that comes against you and threatens to hold you there. It will remove the pain of other people's negative opinions and cancel the lies that Satan whispers in your ear. Joy will help you see life from God's perspective. However things look right now, don't focus on today. Instead, look down the road ahead. It may be Friday, but Sunday is coming. God is working all things for your good. He is turning your setback into a comeback. The joy of the Lord confirms in your heart that you don't have to judge your future by your past.

Chapter Eighteen

LET GOD WRITE
THE FINAL CHAPTER

E verybody is looking for happiness. Whether we are black, white,
brown, yellow, or any shade in between; whether we are rich,
poor, tall, short, Christian or not, we are all searching for a better life.
A fulfilled life is a fundamental human desire. Our drive for fulfillment
frequently leads us into sin because we seek happiness and a better
quality of life from the wrong sources.

In their quest for fulfillment, many people turn to religion.
Unfortunately, religion cannot provide true fulfillment. Essentially,
religion is all about following certain rules in an effort to make an
angry god happy. The road to fulfillment is found not in religion, but
in a personal and intimate relationship with the Lord Jesus Christ.

People who give their lives to the Lord usually do so because
they want a better quality of life than they have had up to now. They
are dissatisfied with life and desperately want to find happiness and
purpose. Life without Christ is empty. Booze, drugs, sex, money,
power—these things may satisfy for a little while, but not long. No

> *"When we trust God in everything, He will give us everything we need."*

matter how much we get, it is never enough.

Only Christ can bring fulfillment to our lives, and only when we are in a personal relationship with Him. Jesus said, *"I came that they might have life, and have it abundantly"* (John 10:10). Life with the Lord is supposed to get better every day. God created us to have a good life. He created us to be fulfilled; He created us to be blessed, to have dreams and visions, and to walk with Him every day. He is all we need. In Matthew 6:33 Jesus said, *"But seek first His kingdom and His righteousness; and all these things shall be added to you."* In other words, when we trust God in everything, He will give us everything we need.

We get ourselves into trouble whenever we go after things or money or power or anything else rather than going after the Lord. Rather than our lives getting better day by day, we fall into negative patterns of thought and behavior and end up in sin. Why do we sin? There are many answers to that question. One answer could be that, for some reason, we believe that it will bring us happiness. We think that the sin will meet a particular need in our lives or solve a particular problem that we have at the moment.

Any time we yield to temptation we are simply trying to meet a legitimate need in our lives in an illegitimate manner. We don't simply wake up and say, "I'm going to do this and see if I can destroy my life." At the time, we actually expect the sin to satisfy a need.

What possible reason could we as Christians have to do something we know is wrong? It is simply that we are not truly convinced that all we need is Jesus. We have a sneaking suspicion in our hearts that there are some needs that we have to meet outside of Him if we are going to be happy. The Bible tells us that Jesus is enough, but we just can't bring ourselves to believe it.

Satan does not need for you to deny Jesus in order to destroy you. All he has to do is get you to believe that what Jesus did for you is not enough. If he can get you to question the Word of God, he can destroy you. Isn't that what he did with Eve? The devil just dropped a little doubt in her ear, "Maybe what God said wasn't enough. Maybe He's holding out on you." If Satan can get you to believe that God's Word is not what *you* need, he can destroy your life.

Jesus Is Enough

You will never find complete fulfillment in your life until you know who you are in Jesus Christ. Contentment will be a stranger to you until you believe that the things that Jesus has done for you are enough. Jesus *is* enough. What problems and heartaches we could avoid if we would simply get that truth through our thick skulls! If Jesus is enough, then you have everything you need when you abide in Him. You don't have to reach for that sin to bring pleasure to your life because you know that in Him you live and move and have your being.

Why is this so hard for us to understand? Here's the problem: Our emotions tell us one thing, while God's Word tells us something else. That's why we cannot allow ourselves to be moved by feeling alone. We have to go back to the Word and find out what God has said about us. Feelings say, "You're a failure." God's Word says, "You can do all things through Christ who strengthens you."

When you look at yourself in the natural, it is easy to feel afraid and incomplete. Don't deny your feelings; they are very real. It is when they do not agree with the Word of God that you have to remind yourself that Jesus is everything you need. He is enough and He makes you enough. In Him you are the righteousness of God.

Righteousness empowers you to overcome the negative patterns in your life. What are the negative factors in your life? Continual financial problems? Ongoing marital difficulties? Trouble on your job? The list could go on and on. Learning to trust the Lord Jesus as sufficient for every need will enable you to overcome and break the negative cycles that hold you back.

If you allow your feelings to lead you to seek fulfillment outside the will of Christ, all you will do is open up your life for a lot of pain.

Any time you look for fulfillment outside of Jesus Christ, you can bet that pain will come into your life. Pain feeds the cycle of destructive patterns of thought and behavior.

Colossians 2:10 says, *"In Him you have been made complete."* A huge part of your maturity as a Christian is reaching the point in your life where you can say, "I am complete in Jesus. He is enough. He is everything." Jesus is the way, the truth, and the life. Nothing outside of Him can ever fulfill you the way He can. If Jesus rose from the dead, don't you think He can help you in any situation you find yourself in?

That Was Then and This Is Now

Romans 8:1 says that there is no condemnation—no condemning sentence—for those who are in Christ Jesus. He is our righteousness. In other words, when God looks at us, He sees the righteousness of Jesus Christ covering us. I don't deserve to be righteous, and neither do you. We don't deserve for anything good to happen to us. Nevertheless, in Christ we are the righteousness of God because when we said, "Jesus, be the Lord of my life," He covered us with His righteousness.

If you have given your life to Christ, there is no condemning sentence over your life. Jesus' blood has declared you "not guilty" and you have been set free. Sure, you failed in the past, but that was then, and this is now. The only one not happy with your new situation is the devil. It's amazing how quickly he will try to draw you back into the very things that God delivered you from.

After we become born again, our past usually chases us vigorously for a while. We often struggle over and over with issues of the past. The truth is, Satan tries to use our past to steal our future. His desire is to rob us of the purpose and destiny that God has for us in life.

The children of Israel left Egypt and all the things of their past. They left behind all their bondage, everything that had held them captive for four hundred years. Even after they left Egypt, their past still chased them in the form of Pharaoh and his army. Their past tried to track them down, recapture them, frighten them, destroy them, and keep them from going into the promised land. God showed them that they needed to stand their ground and face their past once and for all. If they were willing to stand and face their past, He would destroy it for them.

Remember that the children of Israel escaped through the Red Sea, and then the Red Sea covered up their past. In other words, the Red Sea was a type and shadow of the red blood of Jesus Christ that would cover your sins once and for all, never to be found anymore.

Who or what are you running from? What are you trying to escape? What are you afraid of having exposed that would bring shame back into your life? Don't forget that as a born-again believer you are the righteousness of God. You are covered with Jesus' righteousness and there is no condemning sentence hanging over you. God says, "Do not fear, even though your past will run after you. Stand your ground, be silent, and know that the Lord will fight on your behalf." If you will face your enemy—the enemy called your past—God will destroy it right before your very eyes.

> *"The future is all that matters."*

Once you know that you are the righteousness of God, you will never have to feel shame in your life again. That was then, and this is now. The reason the devil has you on his hit list is because of where you are going. He doesn't care where you've been, but he cares where you are going. You *are* going somewhere. God is doing a new thing in your life. He is taking you to a new place.

Don't let the opinions of other people determine where you go or what you do or how you live your life. Their opinions don't matter. Get your past behind you once and for all. Plunge your life under the blood of Jesus, and that "Red Sea" will cover your past.

God wants you to let go of the past so He can do a new thing in your life. He is saying, "Get up and possess the land!" You've got to get up and you've got to fight the good fight of faith. God has said the land is yours, so get up and go after it.

Today you stand at a crossroads. One road leads to your future, the other to your past. Don't follow the road back to your past; there is nothing there for you. The future is all that matters.

The next time someone tries to condemn you to your past, open your mouth and say, "That was then, and this is now." If somebody says, "God can't use somebody like you," say, "That was then, and this is now." "Sure, I used to do drugs, but that was then, and this is now." "Yes, I was a womanizer at one time, but that was then, and this is now." The next time somebody tells you that God cannot use you because you had a baby out of wedlock, say, "Well, yes, I did, but that was then, and this is now." "I did fail in the past, but that was then, and this is now."

If somebody tells you that God can't use you because you went through a divorce, say, "Yeah, I know, man, I did. I didn't like it, I didn't want to do it, and I know it was not God's will for it to happen, but that was then, and this is now. My past is my past, but it's in the past."

Follow Pumbaa's advice to Simba and get your behind in your past. Face forward and let God take you into your future.

The Road Ahead Is All That Matters

In the movie *Cannonball Run* about a madcap cross-country car race, one of the drivers breaks off his rearview mirror just before the race begins and tosses it aside. When someone asks him why, he says, "I don't care what's behind me. What's ahead of me is all that matters."

That's the attitude we should have about life. The past is the past; what's done is done. We can't change where we've been but we can change where we're going. Although we cannot relive all our wasted years (and who would *want* to?), by the grace of God we can reclaim them. We can start over. Our God is the God of second chances.

Stop looking behind you. As long as you insist on rehashing the past, you will condemn yourself to reliving it in the present. You will never escape the past if you continually revisit it. It is time to burn your bridges behind you and say, "The only way to go is forward."

When the prophet Elijah came to anoint Elisha as his successor, Elisha was plowing a field behind twelve pairs of oxen. Upon receiving Elijah's prophetic mantle, Elisha kissed his parents good-bye, burned his plow, and sacrificed the oxen to the Lord (see 1 Kings 19:19–21). This was his way of burning his past—his bridges—and moving into his future.

Let God Write the Final Chapter

You cannot continue doing the same things year after year and expect different results. That's a definition of insanity. Sometimes you have to become so unhappy with being stuck in the past that you burn all the memories and kiss the ashes good-bye. It is time to get out of your rut. Someone said that a rut is only a grave with the ends knocked out. There is a lot of truth in that. The past is dead, so leave it that way.

Death is the realm of darkness, whose lord is Satan. Life is the realm of light, whose Lord is Jesus Christ, the King of kings and Lord of lords. Death stagnates, but life moves ever forward like a swift-flowing stream. If you ever hope to change, you must do things differently than before. Release everything in your past and make plans for a new future.

Not only is God the God of second chances, but He is also the God of new things. As Creator, how could He be anything else? *"Do not call to mind the former things, or ponder things of the past. Behold, I will do something new, now it will spring forth; will you not be aware of it? I will even make a roadway in the wilderness, rivers in the desert"* (Isaiah 43:18–19). The roadway leads to the future; the rivers, to the throne of God.

God wants to do something completely new in your life—something to lead you forward and help you build the future He always planned for you. Before it can happen, however, you need to let go of the past so your hands will be free to take hold of your future. What's done is done. Stop crying over a past that is dead and gone. Quit blaming others for your problems and lack of progress. Stop beating yourself up over your failures. Conduct a funeral and bury your past in the past.

Despite what the devil says, God is not mad at you. He loves you and has a marvelous plan for your life. No matter how much you have messed up or how many years you have wasted, God can still turn your life around and enable you to fulfill His plan and purpose. You can still become all that God wants you to be. His promise is that *"if we confess our sins, He is faithful and righteous to forgive us our sins and to cleanse us from all unrighteousness"* (1 John 1:9).

When Jesus began His public ministry, He was baptized in the Jordan River, which flows into the Dead Sea. In a similar manner, when you were born again, the blood of Jesus washed your sins down the river of life and into the "Dead Sea" of forgetfulness, where He remembers them no more. His blood erased your past—with all its sin, failure, and pain—from heaven's books. If the *Lord* has forgotten your sins, it is high time that *you* did the same.

The Rest of Your Life Is a Blank Page

The time has come to close the preceding chapters of your life and let God write new ones. Do you *really* want to keep pining for the "good old days"? Does it make any sense to continue mourning over a dead romance? What good is there in constantly playing the "what if..." game? They change nothing. Stop flipping back to the front pages of the book and let God show you the rest of the story. He wants to do a new thing for you, and it lies in the future, not the past.

As long as you keep looking back, you can never move forward. With God's help you can cover the memories of your past with the blood of Jesus and start over. The Gospel of Jesus Christ is all about getting a second chance. It is all about starting over. As Charles Howard said of the racing horse Seabiscuit, "We just gave him a chance. Sometimes all somebody needs is a second chance." You can't afford to live in the past any longer or to let anything put your life on hold. Life is too precious and you have too many places to go and too many things to do.

Once you finally get sick and tired of the way things are, you will be in the perfect position for God to turn everything around. He won't move until you are ready to move. Remember, His call is to forget what lies behind, reach forward to what lies ahead, and press toward the prize (see Philippians 3:13–14).

There is no better time than right now to get your past over and done with once and for all. As the old Kenny Rogers song "The Gambler" says, you have to know when to hold 'em, when to fold 'em, when to walk away, and when to run. Bury your past before it buries you. Dry your tears because it is time to move into the promised land. Burn your plow, kill your oxen, and kiss your past goodbye. A whole new future is waiting for you. A new day has arrived, and God wants to do a new thing in your life.

Let God Write the Final Chapter

As long as you are alive and breathing, the final chapter of your life has not been written. Tomorrow is a blank page—a clean, fresh sheet awaiting the scribe's hand. Whose hand will it be? Who will determine the direction of the rest of your story? Will events move predictably to a predetermined conclusion, or will there be a surprise ending?

Only you can decide. If you listen to the voices of your past, things will never change. You will continue to walk in the same old ruts, making the same old decisions and the same old mistakes, trapped on the same old treadmill of guilt, shame, doubt, fear, anger, and bitterness.

A voice is calling to you from the road ahead. It is the voice of the Lord, saying, *"I know the plans that I have for you...plans for welfare and not for calamity to give you a future and a hope"* (Jeremiah 29:11). Listen to His voice. Let God write the final chapters of your life.

With God, nothing is impossible. If you commit your way to the Lord and entrust your future to Him, you will defeat every foe and overcome every obstacle. You can do all things through Christ who strengthens you. With faith, confidence, and joy, you can stand up and say, "My story's not over yet. It may have started off wrong and taken some bad turns, but the Lord is writing the rest of the chapters. Don't judge my future by my past!"

DON'T JUDGE MY FUTURE BY MY PAST

Other Books by
Bishop Dennis Leonard

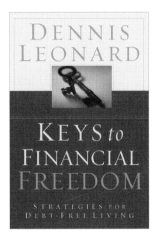

Keys to Financial Freedom

In today's unstable economic landscape, financial insecurity is the constant companion of many struggling to make ends meet. In *Keys to Financial Freedom,* Dennis Leonard offers readers a deliberate choice. Through proven, life-changing strategies, you can learn to assess your financial condition, build new money-management habits, and draw up a financial plan. Then as your wealth and prosperity grow, your faith ignites, and you experience the success of your dreams.

ISBN: 1-880809-20-6
UPC: 88106700008
Hardcover • Retail $25.00

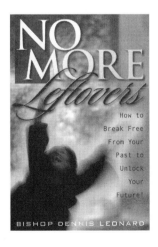

No More Leftovers...
How to Break Free From Your
Past to Unlock Your Future

It's time to let go of past spiritual failures and make plans for a future made strong and prosperous by the power of His might. Living your life just any old way guarantees disappointment. Serve an eviction notice on the devil and tell him you are through with that grasshopper mentality. In *No More Leftovers*, Bishop Dennis Leonard invites you to turn your life around— to experience a promised land—when you live your life God's way.

ISBN: 1-880809-13-3
UPC: 88106700001
Paperback • $15.00

Teaching Series by
Bishop Dennis Leonard

Steps to Overcome Failure

Failing is not necessarily a "bad" thing. Giving up, however, literally pulls the plug on the life-support system of success. You see, success does not just happen. Almost every invention became a success as a result of failure (trial and error). The person simply never gave up. Let Bishop Dennis Leonard show you how past failures can become your stepping-stones to a strong, successful future. Your greatest success could be just over the hill of your present failure.

1534: Failure Is a Stepping-Stone
1535: Failure Leads to Potential
1536: Principles to Overcome Failure
1538: Ten Reasons People Fail

SA-275	4 Audiocassette Series	$20.00
SCD-275	4 CD Series	$30.00
SDVD-275	4 Messages on DVD	$50.00
SV-275	4 Video Series	$50.00

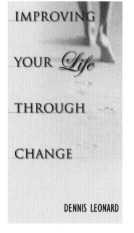

Improving Your Life Through Change

Along with taxes, one the few things certain in life is change. Change is inevitable. How you view that change, though, can either help you or hurt you. Why not take every change that comes your way and use it to improve your life? Why not take control by using it rather than letting it use you? Join Dennis Leonard on the path to "changing" your mind about change!

1530: Changing Improves Your Life
1531: Don't Resist Change
1532: When Life Throws You a Curve
1533: Changing a Negative Mind

SA-274	4 Audiocassette Series	$20.00
SCD-274	4 CD Series	$30.00
SDVD-274	4 Messages on DVD	$50.00
SV-274	4 Video Series	$50.00

Teaching Series by Bishop Dennis Leonard

Crisis: The Turning Point to Your Breakthrough

Do you find it hard to follow through...to change...to make decisions? Don't worry; sooner or later a crisis will come up. If you will let it, that crisis can be your turning point—the spark that changes your life forever. Learn how to use crisis as a springboard to your breakthrough with these eye-opening teachings from Dennis Leonard.

1496: The Crisis Is a Turning Point
1497: Outlasting the Crisis
1499: This Crisis Shall Pass
1501: Trusting God During the Crisis

SA-268	4 Audiocassette Series	$20.00
SCD-268	4 CD Series	$30.00
SDVD-268	4 Messages on DVD	$50.00
SV-268	4 Video Series	$50.00

Finding a Mate

You know deep in your heart that you are ready—you're ready to move on to the next stage in your life—you're ready for marriage and family. Your search is on for the man or woman of your dreams! Finding a mate is one thing; however, connecting with the right mate is another. Join Dennis Leonard as he helps you discover the principles that will make your search successful: integrity, trust, servanthood, communication, and more. *Finding a Mate* will help you make the connection *that lasts a lifetime.*

1540: It's Not Good to Be Alone
1541: Finding a Mate
1542: Looking for Approval
1543: Passing the Mate Test

SA-276	4 Audiocassette Series	$20.00
SCD-276	4 CD Series	$30.00
SDVD-276	4 Messages on DVD	$50.00
SV-276	4 Video Series	$50.00